SPACE WARS

Fact and Fiction

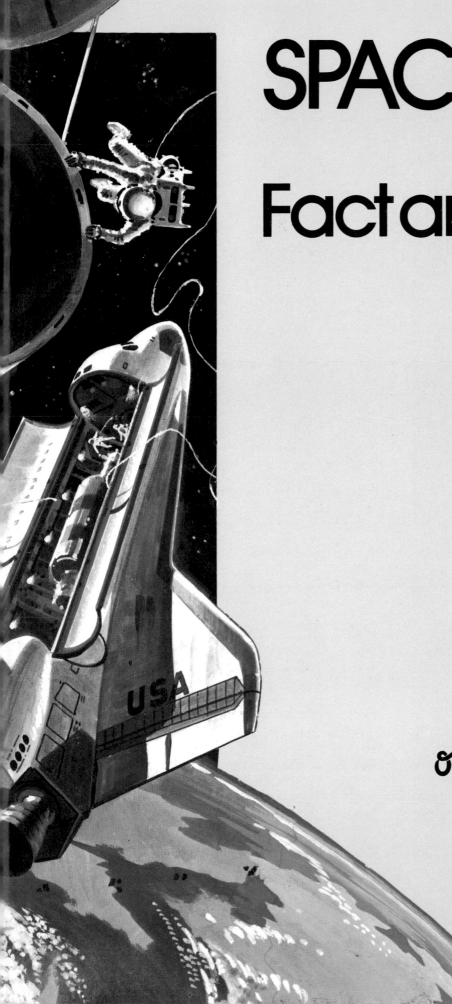

SPACE WARS
Fact and Fiction

octopus

First published by
Octopus Books Limited
59 Grosvenor Street
London W1

© 1980 Octopus Books Limited

**Planned and created by
Martspress Limited
23 Nork Way
Banstead, Surrey**

Printed in Hong Kong

ISBN 0 7064 1350 4

PDO 79/538

Contents

Man Reaches Out

A stone-age man, fleeing from three starving wolves, raced to a tall tree and with the agility of an ape, scaled the tree, pulling himself up powerfully, one hand reaching above the other.

So it has been since man's earliest days and so it will be forever. Man's reaching out will never end. When, at the dawn of this century, he conquered the air with power-driven aircraft, a feat quite beyond the comprehension of a mediaeval man, who could have foreseen that little more than a bare half-century later an astronaut would step down on to the surface of the moon?

And now where? Will boys and girls at school now one day see on a television screen the landing of another dauntless astronaut on another planet in some other galaxy? Who knows? But one thing is certain. In the infinite time of the future, man will never stop reaching out, and discovering new planets.

First Flight to the Edge of Space

Before the history-making day when American astronaut, Neil Armstrong, first set foot on the surface of the Moon many years had been devoted to all the many safeguards and preparations that would ensure not only a safe landing but also a safe return for the astronaut.

Much thought and experimentation had to be devoted to the design of the life-support suits that the astronauts would have to wear. Those suits had then to be tested. This was effected by a dramatic balloon flight to the edge of space ... 21½ miles (83 kilometres) from Earth.

For nine hours, Commander Malcolm D. Ross and Lieutenant Commander Victor A. Prather soared into the heights sitting in an aluminium cage beneath a plastic balloon, filled with helium, which had been launched in the Gulf of Mexico from the aircraft carrier, *USS Antietam*. (Antietam was the name of a famous American Civil War battle.)

At the crest of their climb, they sat in the open gondola for more than two hours with the south-eastern states of America spread out around them like a huge relief map.

'Our aluminium cage offered little protection from the deadly atmospheric conditions around us,' explained Ross afterwards. 'We depended entirely on our space suits and clear plastic face plates. Any failure would have meant instant death. We would almost have exploded.'

Pilots, flying increasingly high, must know the precise capabilities of their suits and a suit that can protect a man above 99 per cent of the Earth's atmosphere is, it was reasoned at the time of the flight in 1961, a major step towards clothing for exploration of the planets.

'Our flight provided the longest, toughest test of space suits ever made under actual operating conditions,' said Ross.

For the dangerous flight, the two daring men used a unique gondola – open but with Venetian

blinds to control the temperature.

The mighty balloon was the biggest successfully tested up to that time. To give some idea of its huge size, its gigantic bag, when filled with helium gas, swelled to a diameter nearly the length of a football field.

Beneath the balloon, the gondola hung from a large parachute which would carry the gondola down if the balloon failed.

Altogether, the balloon, parachute, gondola and trailing aerial made a craft taller than an 80-storey skyscraper.

When the flight began, the balloon climbed rapidly and at 8,230 metres (27,000 feet) the men's space suits began inflating as the pressure outside dropped. At the same time, the temperature fell and when it was minus 94 degrees at 15,850 metres (52,000 feet) the balloon was very brittle.

At 34,668 metres (113,740 feet) the record flight reached its peak – and the descent began at the end of the historic mission into the outer atmosphere, a descent that was to end in tragedy as can be read on page 60.

Rough Justice

'Run that vid-pix slug again,' said the Governor of Prison Satellite Z9. 'Be quick!'

He was a tall man, grey-haired, grey-moustached and thin-faced. His expression – never a jovial one at the best of times – was grim. He tugged at the tight-fitting collar of his black tunic as though it were strangling him.

Lukan, the Assistant Governor, coughed nervously. He watched the technician punch a button on the vid-projector. There was a 'click' and a high-pitched whirring sound. The technician, Lukan noted, was sweating. That wasn't so surprising, under the circumstances. The Governor was known for biting people's heads off at the least provocation; sometimes at no provocation at all. Lukan himself had been the target for at least three blistering verbal attacks since the calamity happened.

Lukan wondered if perhaps calamity wasn't too strong a word to describe the events of yesterday and then rejected the thought. All in all, it wasn't strong enough.

'I said, be quick!'

The Governor's harsh voice cut into his thoughts. The technician fumbled with the projector and flicked a switch. The lights dimmed and the wall opposite the desk became a screen. Lukan's stomach lurched as he saw the now-familiar scene. Catastrophe, he thought gloomily, would be even more apt.

After all, it wasn't every day that ten of the toughest convicts in the Galaxy broke out, hijacked a starcraft and vanished as utterly as though they had never existed.

* * *

The picture on the screen – taken by one of the many security spy-satellites that circled the miniature man-made world of Pris-Sat Z9 – was a close-up of part of a new extension the Governor had ordered to be constructed. There were over 3,000 men imprisoned on the titanium-treated steel globe and every six months saw a new intake of convicts arriving on the starships. Space inside the satellite was at a premium.

All the Pris-Sats were self-supporting. There were hydroponic farms for food, and vast workshops where the cons sweated it out in shifts. There were leisure areas too, but that didn't mean that serving time was any sort of picnic. Only the most violent criminals were sentenced to spend the rest of their lives on the Pris-Sats and the work was hard.

Hardest of all was space-construction, outside the satellite itself.

Lukan gazed at the picture on the screen. The spy-camera had focussed on a big man in a pressure-suit, floating on a safety line near naked girders. Lukan knew the man to be Carl Dorker, a violent but cunning gang-leader who had been convicted of space piracy.

In the background could be seen a couple of small shuttle craft, one of them lugging a power-riveter, with two cons hauling a lock-shaft after it. Far beyond that – probably about 500 spacials – was the starship from Earth, with a new batch of convicts ready to be transferred to the prison satellite. Below could be seen the strange rushing cloud patterns of the dead planet Demeter.

All Pris-Sats hung over dead planets, especially selected by the Terran prison commission. There had never yet been a break-out from any of them but if there was, it was thought that the cons would make for the nearest planet. No one stood much chance of survival on a dead world and escapers could be rounded up with comparative ease on its inhospitable surface.

Lukan was automatically counting the seconds as he watched the scene. He saw Dorker pull a high tensile rod into place in the tangle of steelwork and saw the two shuttles drifting nearer and nearer, on low power.

Suddenly, the starship in the far background vanished in a blaze of white light. Lukan had been ready for the searing explosion but he still winced as the huge ship burst apart soundlessly. It was as though a new sun had abruptly appeared in the night-darkness of space to blaze for a few brief seconds before dying into nothingness. As it died, there came the awful aftermath. The two shuttles spun out of control. A man – his pressure-suit torn to shreds – spiralled past in the vacuum of space. Lukan saw bits of steel framework on the right hand side of the screen buckle and twist and Dorker's legs were kicking out as though the man was being wrenched away from the girder he was clinging to, by a mighty invisible hand.

Then the scene shimmered crazily and the screen went blank.

The lights went up in the Governor's office. Lukan blinked and shook his head dazedly.

'I still don't understand how Dorker survived,' said the Governor. His fingers beat a steady tattoo on the alloy top of his desk. 'As we know, the spy-camera went dead at that point – by all rights, Dorker ought to have done the same. The blast should have torn him right out of the orbit of our satellite and sent him into deep space, along with the rest of the debris. And yet . . . .'

'We don't even know why the starship exploded,' Lukan broke in. 'Sabotage . . . .?'

The Governor shook his head irritably.

'Fission reactor blew out . . . unstable booster energisers . . . it could have been any one of half a dozen reasons. That's not the point, Lukan.' He smacked his palm down on the desk-top angrily. 'The point is that the ship exploded. The force of the explosion destroyed half of the new-girder erections on the port side of the Prison Satellite and blew the communication and alarm systems to dust. For nearly an hour our security network was useless!'

Lukan breathed heavily.

'An hour was all they needed. . . .'

'Less!' snapped the Governor. 'During the aftermath of the blast, there was so much chaos down there that ten convicts were able to overpower the guards at docking station B13, board a small cruiser and take off!'

Lukan shifted uncomfortably in his seat.

'And the cruiser had star-drive,' he said.

The Governor banged the desk-top again.

'Precisely! And they have used it! Here on the very edge of the known Galaxy. Out there' – he waved a hand – 'is uncharted space. And that's where they've gone. It would take a full-scale expedition to locate them.' He glared round at Lukan. 'Give me the names again.'

The Assistant Governor viewed a clipboard.

'Most of them were from Earth. There was Carl Dorker, for a start . . . .'

The Governor grunted. Both men were remembering the jeering voice of the big man over the communications room speaker system, just before the cruiser had de-materialised into hyper-space.

I've beaten you, suckers – beaten justice! You'll never see me again!

It had been a shock to learn that Dorker had survived the terrible blast.

Lukan went on: 'Schmidt, Ellison, Wilde, Drozsh – the Beakman from Bazra – Dowson, Ellis, Harlan, Gort and Flecker.'

'A vicious bunch,' muttered the Governor. His fingers tugged at his grizzled moustache. 'Except, of course, for Flecker . . . .'

'Flecker . . . .' repeated Lukan. He bit his lower lip worriedly. 'Ironic, in a way, sir.'

For once, the Governor didn't snap at his sub-

ordinate. Instead, he nodded.

'Very,' he said heavily. 'Eye-witnesses tell me that Flecker wasn't actually one of Dorker's original party but just happened to be down near the docking station when Dorker grabbed the ship.'

He pulled a piece of paper towards him and gazed at it broodingly. 'Ironic that Flecker should break out the very day I get an A-1 Priority signal from Earth saying that Flecker had been wrongly convicted. That we were to send him back to Earth on the first available trans-

port. That he's been given a free pardon.'

* * *

'The sooner we make planet-fall, the better'.

On the command-bridge of the hijacked cruiser, the man who said this was scowling down at a figure lying sprawled on the floor.

The speaker turned and looked across the control-room to where a group of men were standing, sullen-faced and tense, by a computer bank. 'You're getting space-happy, Dorker. There was no need to shoot the guy.'

Carl Dorker hefted a hand-laser in his right hand. He was a big man with brutal features. He glared at the speaker.

'And you're getting squeamish, Dowson. Schmidt didn't seem to realise who's calling the shots on this ship. He thought he could take over. He was wrong. Are you thinking you would like to take over . . . .?'

Dowson, on the small side, with a thin, ferret-like face, sneered.

'No way, Dorker. I came along for the ride. All I will say is that if you keep knocking off your crew' – and Dowson glanced to where another crumpled body lay, on the steps leading down to the lower navigation room – 'there soon won't be anyone left but you.'

The big man made to step forward.

'You little runt! I've had about as much as I can take of your . . . .'

'That's enough!'

One of the men in the group suddenly stepped forward. He was younger than the others by a few years, with crisp, curly hair. He, too, held a laser pistol loosely in his right hand. 'Are you crazy, Dorker? Maybe Dowson's right. Maybe you do want to kill us all off!'

The big man turned. On his face was a wolfish grin that held no trace of humour.

'You, too, Flecker! Now you're poking your oar in. The guy who shouldn't be here at all. The guy who was wrongly convicted – says you! Maybe I'll deal with you as well . . . .'

'Listen, Dorker – you're sick!' Flecker's voice was urgent now. 'I reckon you must have caught a massive dose of radiation after the blast you survived. You're not thinking straight. There are medical facilities on this ship and . . . .'

'No!' Dorker screamed out the word. 'No one sticks any needles into Carl Dorker – do you hear? No one. . . .'

At that moment, a series of high-pitched bleeps cut across what he was saying and the men in the bridge swung round to stare at the computer-control on the other side of the room. 'Look!' It was the Beakman from the planet Bazra, who pointed a clawed hand shakily at the scanner-screen on the right of the computer facia. On it could be seen a reddish ball, hanging in the blackness of space.

'A planet!' Dowson turned to one of his companions, a tall white-haired man. 'Wilde, you know how to work the computer. Check it out!'

'Not quite an Earth-type planet,' he reported. 'Air's dense – lot of dust in it, as far as I can tell – but breathable.'

'Life?' queried Dorker harshly.

Wilde frowned; pressed more buttons. 'Can't make it out. Seem to be city formations . . . centres of population – but I'm not getting any positive readings on humanoids.' He glanced up at the computer. 'Could be I'm punching wrong codes into the computer. I haven't touched one of these for years.'

'If there are cities, there are people,' snapped Dorker. He grinned. 'And if there are people, there's loot!' He jabbed a finger at Gort, an ex-pilot who was navigating the ship. 'Take her in!'

* * *

The eight men stared around them.

Above, the sky was a lofty vault of orange-red clouds. The air was thick and heavy, clogged with the reddish dust the convicts kicked up whenever they moved. It was a bleak, inhospitable landscape, rocky and parched. Long canyons stretched away to one side, beneath high, serrated rocky peaks and ridges; behind them red mountains reared up high into the sullen red sky.

Flecker glanced at the two shuttle-craft sitting on a flat stretch of rock and then gazed up at the cloud-cover. Up there, he knew, orbiting just above the planet's atmosphere – or what passed for atmosphere on this seemingly dead world – was the empty cruiser. It seemed crazy to him to stay on this barren planet, when they could simply take off again for another more friendly world.

As he thought this, he was suddenly aware of Drozsh, near him. The Beakman was clutching at his scaly throat, coughing and gasping. His tiny green eyes were almost closed; his huge beak quivering and snorting. Suddenly he crashed to the ground. Flecker sprang to his side.

'What the heck's the matter with him?' snarled Dorker.

Flecker looked up grimly.

'Dead!' he said tersely. 'The atmosphere was too much for him. The sensitive membranes in his beak got clogged up with all this darn dust in the air. Don't forget, Bazra's a watery planet, with a sharp, clean atmosphere.'

Dorker shrugged.

'One less mouth to feed,' he said callously. 'Lucky we aren't so sensitive.'

At that moment, there was a low cry from behind them. Flecker got to his feet and turned. About fifty yards away, Harlan was peering over a jumble of rocks at something beyond. He beckoned urgently and the six men moved quickly towards him.

Beyond the rocks was a steepish slope that curved away out of sight below. On the slope were a number of what looked like patterned balls, of all shapes and sizes. At this distance, Flecker couldn't make out whether they were rocks or some sort of vegetable matter – but in any case this wasn't important. What was far more interesting – even sinister – was the figure that stood on the slope beside the balls.

'Mek-man of some kind,' whispered Dowson. 'Means there are people here, of some kind or other. Robots don't build themselves!'

The robot was made of some sort of hard dull alloy. It had two heavy-duty arms and stood on thick, bulky legs. Its 'face' was covered by a dome of plasti-glass and underneath could be seen an intricate brain structure from which

protruded three glowing 'eyes'. It was holding one of the smaller balls in its metal pincer and a beam of green light shone down from one of the 'eyes' on to it.

'A work-mek, I reckon,' Flecker said, standing up. 'Should be harmless.'

Instantly, the robot's head lifted and a squawking gabble rang out. The green beam cut out and in its place was a yellow ray, which played around the startled men.

'It's attacking!' yelled Dorker, lifting his laser-gun and firing it. 'Harlan, Ellison, the rest of you – nail it!'

The laser-beam seared the dusty air and struck the ground inches away from the robot. Abruptly, the yellow ray winked off and a red beam lashed out, striking rocks in front of the

convicts and blasting them to powder. Again the red beam stabbed out and Harlan and Ellison shrieked aloud as it struck them. They were hurled backwards, away from the lip of the slope.

'You lunatic, Dorker!' roared Flecker. 'Throwing a laser at it has turned it lethal!'

The sizzling red ray swept round again.

'Down!' Flecker howled, as he dived at Dowson, hurling him to the ground just as the red ray seared the air where he had been.

Dowson spat dust out of his mouth and gripped Flecker's arm.

'That's the second time you've saved me,' he muttered. 'I won't forget it. Listen,' he went on urgently, 'I must tell you . . . .'

But at that moment the squawking gabble from the robot was cut off abruptly and a loud hollow voice boomed out across the slope. 'Beings! We have assimilated your speech patterns. You are now in no danger. The death of two of your number was an unfortunate error. We regret this. Our servo-mek, through whom we are communicating with you, will bring you to our city. Please follow him in your craft.'

The convicts crouched below the ridge.

'It's a trick,' snarled Dorker. 'Once we move, that tin-can killer will waste us!'

Flecker stood up and pointed to where the robot was now rising up gently into the air.

'Don't be stupid, Dorker,' he said. 'It could pulverise us anyhow, whether we get up or stay here. We might as well follow it.'

* * *

The city stretched away from them. Tier upon tier of towering structures; some of glass, some of alloy that shone like silver, some of a black construction.

As they neared the vast city, the sky darkened, turning a deep purple. Fork lightning shredded the darkness; rain hissed down.

'Crazy atmosphere,' muttered Wilde.

'Artificial, I'd guess,' said Flecker, gazing out at the rain, which, even as he watched was dying to a drizzle and soon ceased completely. 'The rain only fell over the city and the surrounding hills. Pretty sophisticated weather-making machines somewhere down there.'

They landed on a wide silver-paved plaza, near a sky-high erection. The robot who had led them disappeared into the building.

The five convicts gazed around them. Flecker was suddenly aware of a silence that was total, absolute . . . sinister.

'I don't like it,' he muttered.

'Scared?' sneered Dorker. 'I'm not surprised.'

The big man's eyes glittered feverishly. 'Still, I'm glad I brought you along. Heck of a joke, that – that I hike you millions of light-years away from the Pris-Sat just when you might have had some, uh . . . good news.' He laughed jeeringly.

Flecker grabbed him by the throat.

'What do you mean by that, Dorker?'

In an instant, the big man had clawed for his laser-gun and was dragging it up.

'Don't touch me! I'll shoot you like I shot Ellis and Schmidt! I'll . . . .'

'Hold it, Dorker!' It was Dowson, laser in hand. 'There are only five of us left, pal. The more guys you knock off, the less chance we have of defending ourselves against . . . .'

Flecker turned contemptuously away from the big convict.

'There are no humans here,' he interrupted. 'You can't even hear the darn machines – the robots. So what happened to everybody? Where did the people who built that robot go?'

'Yeah,' said Dowson. 'And who was the guy who spoke to us through the robot?'

As if on cue they heard a faint humming sound and glanced up at the sky.

Floating down through the still air from the top of the glass-fronted building were a number of shiny silver spheres. They each had two bulbous eyes. Each had six slender appendages that ended in a kind of flipper; two above the eyes, two below the grille and two sprouting from the rear. The flippers waved lazily in the air as the globes hovered above the astonished heads of the convicts.

A silvery, slightly echoing voice shrilled: 'You may not leave our world.'

Dorker gave a bull-like roar and fired at the leading globe. Nothing happened. Dorker gaped.

Flecker glanced around. He was suddenly aware of a gossamer-like tingling on his face and hands. The very air around the convicts seemed to be sparkling.

'You are now within a raised ion-field and your primitive weapons are useless. They will only work when we lift the field.'

'What is this?' snapped Flecker. 'Who are you? Why do you want to hold us here?'

'You are the first humanoids to land here for . . . .' the voice paused for a second, then continued '. . . . 238,000 years, by your reckoning. The race who created us died out many aeons before that but we have been programmed to continue our tasks. Our servo-meks continue to rove this planet, testing ore, vegetable matter, rock samples – one such you disturbed earlier.'

Flecker shook his head disbelievingly.

'As the years have passed, the central brain that controls the computer-mind that was originally programmed – of which we are merely autonomous neural extensions – has wished for a humanoid specimen to study. We are eager to develop but to do that we must ponder on the type of being that brought us into existence. It seems to us that the type must, of necessity, be a leader – a survivor. There are only five of you beings. It is clear that one being must emerge above the rest – in cunning, speed, intelligence . . . .'

The silvery voice faded. Then:

'Do I get you right?' said Flecker. 'Are you saying we have to fight each other – and . . . . and the winner takes all?'

There was no answer.

Dorker rubbed the side of his face. An insane grin disfigured his face.

Suddenly, Flecker realised his flesh was no longer tingling. 'They've cut off the ion-field!' he gasped.

After that, events moved fast. Flecker was pulling at his gun to stop Dorker but the big man, laughing like a madman, was already firing. He heard Dowson yell 'Look out!' and felt the little man crash into him, dragging him towards the ground. Then he felt a blow like the kick of a mammoth and both of them were hurtling through the air. Flecker landed on the paving stones with Dowson on top of him. A breath-robbing pain seized him.

* * *

He saw Dorker standing alone in the centre of the plaza, laughing madly.

He heard the silvery voice again.

'Excellent. You are clearly the leader. You have despatched the other beings swiftly. We will learn much from you.'

'Yeah!' said Dorker. 'And then I can start learning, too. The only human on a planet run by robots! Yeah, I'll be a leader all right. The stuff you've got here – why, I could run the Galaxy with it!'

Flecker saw two silver strands shoot out from above the speaker-grille on the leading globe, with what appeared to be two tiny cups at the end of each strand. Dazedly, he thought they looked like suction pads.

The cups struck Dorker on the forehead and stuck there. The strands became taut as the globe abruptly rose higher. Dorker was jerked off his feet.

'That is an incorrect assessment,' said the globe. 'You will never leave this planet. We will study you. It will take many years but it will, we know, prove rewarding. We must discover exactly how you function – each part of you . . . . every nerve and muscle.'

Dorker was dragged higher and higher into the air, until he disappeared into the top of the glass tower.

The other globes hovered for a few seconds then drifted out of sight.

Flecker crawled from under Dowson's dead weight. The little man had saved him from the full force of Dorker's blast. Gort and Wilde were dead, but Dowson's eye-lids fluttered.

'Come on,' croaked Flecker.

Dowson feebly shook his head.

'Done . . . for, kid. We're . . . quits, now. Got to tell you . . . at the Pris-Sat, Dorker heard . . . you had been given . . . a free pardon. Told us not . . . to tell you. Thought it was . . . funny. Now . . . you know . . . .'

His head flopped back.

Flecker looked down at him. On an impulse, he lifted Dowson gently and hobbled towards the nearest shuttlecraft.

As he punched out a take-off code on the console, he thought about Dorker.

Dorker had jeered at justice – had thought he had escaped it. But his sentence now was worse than any he would have had to endure on a Pris-Sat. Justice, of a sort, had finally caught up with Carl Dorker.

The shuttle lifted off – lanced high into the vault of the heavens towards the waiting cruiser.

They called it the "Grape Fruit"

Satellite! Before 31 January 1958, the word was not familiar to school children. Today the word is common-place and seven-year-olds playing ball in their back gardens have heard the word used countless times.

The reason for this? And the significance of the date 31 January 1958? Well, that was the day that the American scientists of the US Defence Department launched into orbit their first satellite, named Explorer I.

Old dictionaries define the word 'satellite' as 'a secondary planet revolving round a greater planet, as the moon does around the Earth.' Now there is a second meaning to the word, for today man-made unmanned satellites are orbiting Earth at apogees (distant points from the Earth) of hundreds of miles.

Explorer I orbited Earth at an apogee of 585 kilometres (364 miles) and a perigree (its nearest point to Earth) of 294 kilometres (182.7 miles).

After being launched aboard a Jupiter C rocket, Explorer I reported to Earth the existence of a radiation belt about the globe now called the Van Allen Belt. It was named after a scientist at the American State University of Iowa who provided the scientific instruments within the satellite.

From the moment the first satellite was launched, the world at large became aware that space exploration was now a definite possibility. Perhaps that is one reason why the Americans have always regarded their satellite Explorer I with a certain affection, manifested by its nickname of 'Grape Fruit.' It weighed only 6 kilogrammes (13¼ lbs).

The years that have passed since Explorer I first shot into orbit have proved epoch-making. Manned craft, space dockings, moon landings and satellite reportings on other planets have written pages of excitement and adventure into our history books.

Explorer I's life came to an end in 1970 when it re-entered the Earth's atmosphere and was burned up. It may have gone forever but its contribution to the history of the conquest of space will last as long as our Earth endures.

SPACE CADET

Nelson's famous flag-ship the *Victory* has been well preserved over the centuries and today it is due to be dedicated by the people of Britain to the noble and worthy cause of Inter-Stellar World Peace. The Director of Space Force I will attend the ceremony. Armed police parade Victory Square in Portsmouth as the dawn sun lightens the sky. The date is 21 October, 2805 AD, 1,000 years after the battle of Trafalgar in which the ship *Victory* played its glorious part.

Reveille is being blown at the Royal Space Academy just as it has been blown ever since the force was first founded in 2015 AD.

It has long been the tradition that every class at the academy is named after a bygone space project. The third year cadets belong to the 'Ranger' class. The first Ranger cadet awake that morning was Tom Bolt, who was a coward and a bully.

There was one cadet Tom Bolt hated with every ounce of his soul, and this morning Bolt had arranged a most unpleasant surprise for his enemy . . . an early bath in dirty waste fuel.

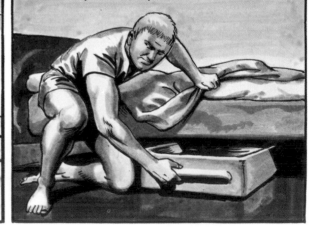

Moving swiftly, for he had only a few moments before the rest of the cadets awoke, Bolt hauled the bath to the bed of the cadet he hated. 'It's all set up! Now to push him into it,' he muttered.

Tom Bolt pushed with all his might . . . suddenly and powerfully . . . expecting to roll his hated enemy clean out of the bed and into the bath of smelly black oil. But . . .

. . . the bed was empty except for three pillows. The next instant, a pair of hands grasped the class bully by the ankles.

The astonished Tom Bolt was up-ended across the bed . . .

. . . to splash into the sticky horrible mess he had so carefully prepared on the previous evening.

Dazedly, Tom Bolt peered up into the laughing blue eyes of his most hated enemy . . . young Jason January, Cadet Captain of the Rangers.

'I spotted you setting that trap last night,' Jason grinned. 'My alarm wristwatch woke me in time to put pillows in my bed.'

'All right! You win this time, January,' snarled Bolt. 'But just watch out. One day, I'll get even with you!'

Bolt's revenge was to happen in very strange circumstances . . . but now we move to another planet, the lair of a fierce and ruthless band of space pirates.

The pirate leader was a brutal giant named Hercules Canute. For some time now, he had been planning nothing less than the audacious theft of the *Victory*.

'Get ready, men,' Canute ordered. 'We strike today. And they'll only get the *Victory* back when the British release those 200 men of mine they captured last year.'

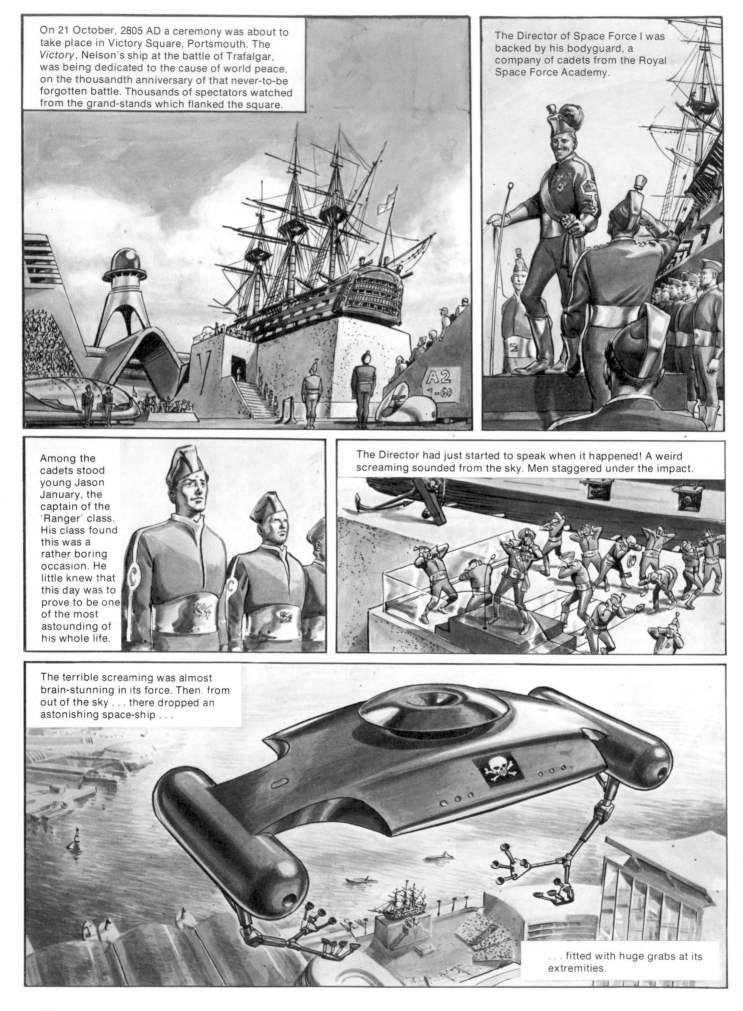

On 21 October, 2805 AD a ceremony was about to take place in Victory Square, Portsmouth. The *Victory*, Nelson's ship at the battle of Trafalgar, was being dedicated to the cause of world peace, on the thousandth anniversary of that never-to-be forgotten battle. Thousands of spectators watched from the grand-stands which flanked the square.

The Director of Space Force I was backed by his bodyguard, a company of cadets from the Royal Space Force Academy.

Among the cadets stood young Jason January, the captain of the 'Ranger' class. His class found this was a rather boring occasion. He little knew that this day was to prove to be one of the most astounding of his whole life.

The Director had just started to speak when it happened! A weird screaming sounded from the sky. Men staggered under the impact.

The terrible screaming was almost brain-stunning in its force. Then. from out of the sky . . . there dropped an astonishing space-ship . . .

. . . fitted with huge grabs at its extremities.

The giant grabs clamped on to either end of the *Victory* and the giant space-ship soared away with the priceless vessel.

When the stunning screaming ceased, Jason January saw what was happening to Nelson's flag-ship. He bounded forward.

Jason grasped the anchor of the *Victory* – and was swiftly plucked skywards.

Aboard the space-ship, Hercules Canute chuckled. Jason was hidden from view.

Towed higher and higher into the sky as the space-ship gathered speed, Jason January summoned up the strength to pull himself on to the anchor. Then, in sheer desperation, he began a perilous and muscle-testing climb up the length of the anchor cable.

Noting the skull-and-crossbones insignia, Jason realised that the raid had been carried out by a band of pirates who had been terrorizing the world.

'Last year, the Royal Space Force captured 200 sky pirates,' muttered Jason. 'Lord Nelson's ship has been hi-jacked as an act of revenge.'

Jason knew that the pirates would not have stolen *Victory* in so spectacular a way had they intended to destroy it. A trip to the pirates' lair in outer space would break up the timbers of the old ship.

They must be taking it to a secret hide-out somewhere on the surface of the Earth.

Up the anchor cable clambered Jason until he was able to crawl through the anchor hawse-hole.

Aboard the space-grappler, Hercules Canute, the leader of the space-pirates, was roaring with glee at the success of his well-planned and audacious scheme.

'Now for the island of Wu-Cheng,' he bellowed. 'The British will never suspect that the *Victory* will be hidden somewhere half-way round the world!'

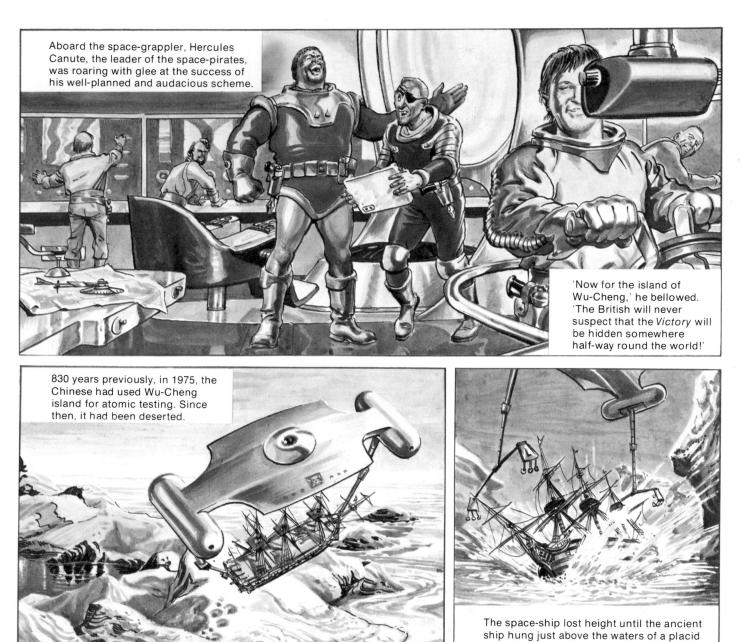

830 years previously, in 1975, the Chinese had used Wu-Cheng island for atomic testing. Since then, it had been deserted.

Just 30 minutes after leaving Portsmouth, Canute's mighty space-craft was descending on to the island of Wu-Cheng.

The space-ship lost height until the ancient ship hung just above the waters of a placid lake. Then the two great claws opened.

Meanwhile, Canute and some of his men were descending from the space-ship to inspect their prize.

Only the fact that the timbers of the old vessel had been well preserved prevented it from falling apart on impact.

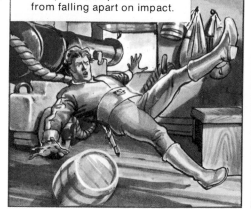

Below decks, Jason struck his head as the ship hit the water, and was knocked unconscious.

'You have imprisoned 200 of my men! Release them – and I will return the *Victory* to you.' This was to be the bargain offered to Britain by Hercules Canute, space pirate of the 29th century.

While Hercules Canute and his men prowled above, Jason lay unconscious where he had been struck senseless.

If Jason was discovered, he would be killed. Already, one pirate was about to descend the hatch-way.

But suddenly the surface of the lake began to ripple in ever-increasing circles, and an enormous shape could dimly be glimpsed rising from the green depths. 'Look!' shouted one of the pirates. 'What's that?'

While Hercules Canute and his men gazed at the lake in horrified disbelief, a gigantic and fearsome monster broke the surface of the water. Its red eyes glowed balefully as it beheld the ancient ship, and its great jaws opened wide to display rows of razor-sharp teeth.

Canute and his pirates gaped in sheer terror. They had not known that atomic tests in the late 20th century had done strange things to the island. A rebirth of prehistoric animals was one of them.

Bolts from Canute's space-blaster merely bounced off the monster.

A terrified pirate croaked into his walkie-talkie. 'Snatch up the ship – or we'll be killed!' he gasped.

A few minutes later, Canute's sky-grappler answered the call and came swooping down out of the sky.

The pirates aboard the sky-grappler acted promptly. Down came the claws, and Canute and his ruffians leapt to grasp them.

Recovering his senses and stumbling up on to the deck, Jason January found himself gazing into the gaping, slavering jaws of what he saw to be a prehistoric monster.

27

Standing transfixed by sheer horror on the wooden deck of the *Victory*, Jason January thought that his last moment had come. It seemed certain that he was destined to be seized by the long glittering teeth of the hideous sea-monster. And, once he was held fast in the grip of those jaws, no power on earth could save him!

But, as Jason stood rooted to the spot, the head of the massive beast suddenly turned away from him. A powerful swirl of the green waters of the lake had attracted its attention. Its long neck swayed to the left as it sensed that it was being threatened from the rear.

Ploughing through the waters of the lagoon came another nightmare creature . . . just one more of nature's grim jests caused by man's atomic tests of the 20th century.

It was obvious from the behaviour of both animals that they were deadly enemies. Soon, they were locked in combat.

Standing behind the ancient mast, Jason watched the battle of the giants. 'Whichever wins will turn to attack the *Victory* – and me!' he muttered.

Suddenly he knew what he had to do. Stacked below decks on the ship were cannon balls and gun-powder – used when Nelson fought his great battle.

It was back-breaking work to manhandle the massive guns and load them with powder and shot. But, working at top speed, Jason soon had all eight guns primed and ready for action.

Crouched behind the guns, the cadet watched the final stages of the life-and-death struggle. Soon, one head emerged triumphant from the water, a great barbed tail lashed the surface to foam – and a pair of hateful eyes turned towards the ancient ship.

As the beast turned to rend the ship to matchwood, tho cadet opened fire – with gun after gun.

One by one, the guns of *Victory* barked their leaden message of defiance, as in glorious days of yore.

The iron roundshot rebounded from the monster's iron·hide like so many harmless peas – but the noise and the stabbing flame unnerved the creature. Baffled, it swerved wildly and, diving deep beneath the surface, disappeared from Jason's sight.

Jason was jubilant . . . but he knew that he had only won a brief respite. The beast would return . . . or one like it.

Then he saw it . . . a pocket walkie-talkie dropped by one of the pirates. He picked up the instrument immediately . . .

. . . and set it to the S.O.S. channel. 'Jason January calling!' he snapped.

At the Space Force Academy in Portsmouth, Sparks Springfield, an amateur radio enthusiast, was keeping his comrades awake in their dormitory.

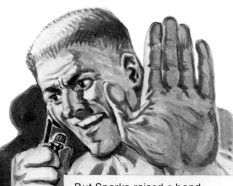

'Turn that squawk-box off, Sparks!' yelled an irate cadet. 'Get yourself some beauty-sleep . . . you need it!'

But Sparks raised a hand to call for silence. 'There's an S.O.S. coming through,' he gasped. 'I think it's from Jason!'

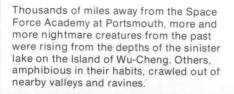

Thousands of miles away from the Space Force Academy at Portsmouth, more and more nightmare creatures from the past were rising from the depths of the sinister lake on the Island of Wu-Cheng. Others, amphibious in their habits, crawled out of nearby valleys and ravines.

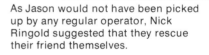

The bait which attracted all these weird and fearsome beasts was Lord Nelson's little flagship *Victory*, floating alone and unprotected in the centre of the lagoon.

'Send help,' cried Jason urgently into his transmitter. 'I will soon be attacked by monsters – and the space pirates who stole *Victory*!'

Back in the 'Ranger' class dormitory, all the cadets were gathered around Sparks Springfield. 'Tell Jason to hold on!' cried one. 'Tell him we'll send help!'

As Jason would not have been picked up by any regular operator, Nick Ringold suggested that they rescue their friend themselves.

'We can do it,' cried Nick. 'We can recover the *Victory* for Britain, and save Jason, too. Come on! Let's go!'

Only Tom Bolt, the class bully, refused to join the rescue party. 'I'm not risking my life!' he growled.

The rest of the eager cadets swiftly donned their space gear. With sullen eyes, the bully sat and watched them go.

Explaining their plan to two of their own classmates who were guarding the 'Ranger' class's space craft, the cadets swarmed aboard the sleek and glittering ship.

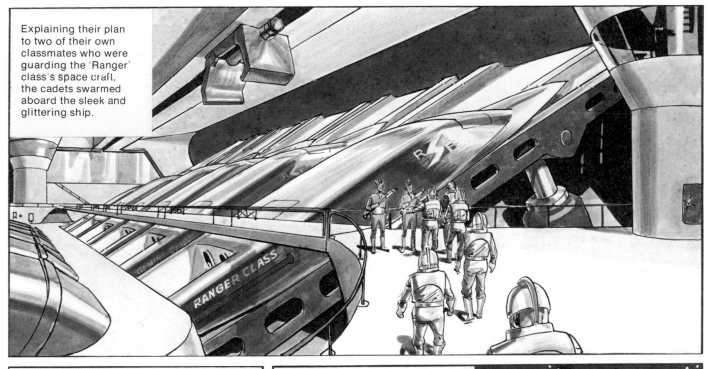

Soon, the dull roar of booming jets filled the hangar as the cadets primed and tested the atomic engines. All were busy at their tasks – too busy to notice Tom Bolt climbing into a spare equipment locker.

A cunning plan was forming in Tom Bolt's mind – a plan to get his comrades into dire trouble – and to collect all the credit for recovering the hi-jacked *Victory*.

Five minutes later, the powerful space craft roared off into the night sky, trailing behind it a bright plume of smoke and red-tinged white-hot flame.

Meanwhile, aboard the space-grappler, Canute, the brutal leader of the space pirates, was shouting at his men. 'Monsters or no monsters, we must retrieve the *Victory* from that island!' he shouted. 'I vow it, by the moons of Saturn!'

'Six men will be dropped into the lagoon in the armoured fighting capsule,' bellowed Canute. 'While they deal with the monsters, we will lift the *Victory* with our twin grapplers!'

Trailing the armoured capsule beneath it, the giant space craft swooped down towards the lagoon!

Zooming low over the deserted Island of Wu-Cheng, Hercules Canute's gigantic space ship skirted the *Victory* and skimmed across that part of the green lagoon where the bulk of the savage sea-and-land-monsters had gathered. Spike-toothed jaws gaped wide and armoured tails lashed in anger.

Inside the armoured fighting capsule, Canute's six chosen men looked down at the creatures below them and quaked with fear. 'We'll stand no chance,' wailed one. 'They'll tear our craft to shreds!'

Aboard the *Victory* Jason January looked up into the sky with foreboding. The unexpected return of Canute and his pirates had come as a grim shock.

In the control cabin of his mighty space-grappler, the pirate-leader gave the order: 'Drop the fighting capsule into the lagoon!'

The capsule containing the unfortunate six men fell with a resounding splash among the milling monsters, and was at once attacked by them.

It was typical of the merciless Canute that he had no plans to recover the fighting capsule. He would sacrifice his men to regain control of the *Victory*.

While the sea-creatures' attention was fixed on the capsule, Hercules Canute manoeuvred his sky-grappler low over Lord Nelson's tiny flag-ship.

Crouched behind the mast, Jason watched with a numb feeling of helplessness as the grabs closed on the ancient hull. Then six pirates came swarming down.

Canute was putting these men aboard the ship to guard her when she landed again in a safer haven.

At this moment a sleek shape streaked down from the stratosphere upon the Island of Wu-Cheng. It was the Rangers' class space craft which had raced halfway across the world in answer to Jason January's call for help!

Space cadet Nick Ringold was in command. He saw the pirate craft about to snatch up the *Victory*. 'Fire a warning shot close to them!'

An instant later, a well-aimed shot from the Rangers' disintegrating cannon streaked only yards from the nose of Hercules Canute's ugly craft, causing panic aboard her.

Hercules Canute gave the order to cast off the old ship . . . and the pirates left on the deck of the *Victory* yelled with alarm when they realized that they were being left to their fate.

Thrilled by the familiar shape of the space craft turning to attack the pirate ship again, Jason forgot his own peril and ran forward in exultation. 'Come on, Rangers!' he shouted at the top of his voice. 'Get at 'em again. Knock them clean out of the sky!'

He checked himself . . . too late. The six pirates turned on him menacingly. Someone was going to pay for their being marooned on the *Victory* in a lagoon . . . and that someone was going to be the space cadet.

Jason January was in a tight spot . . . one of the tightest spots he had ever faced.

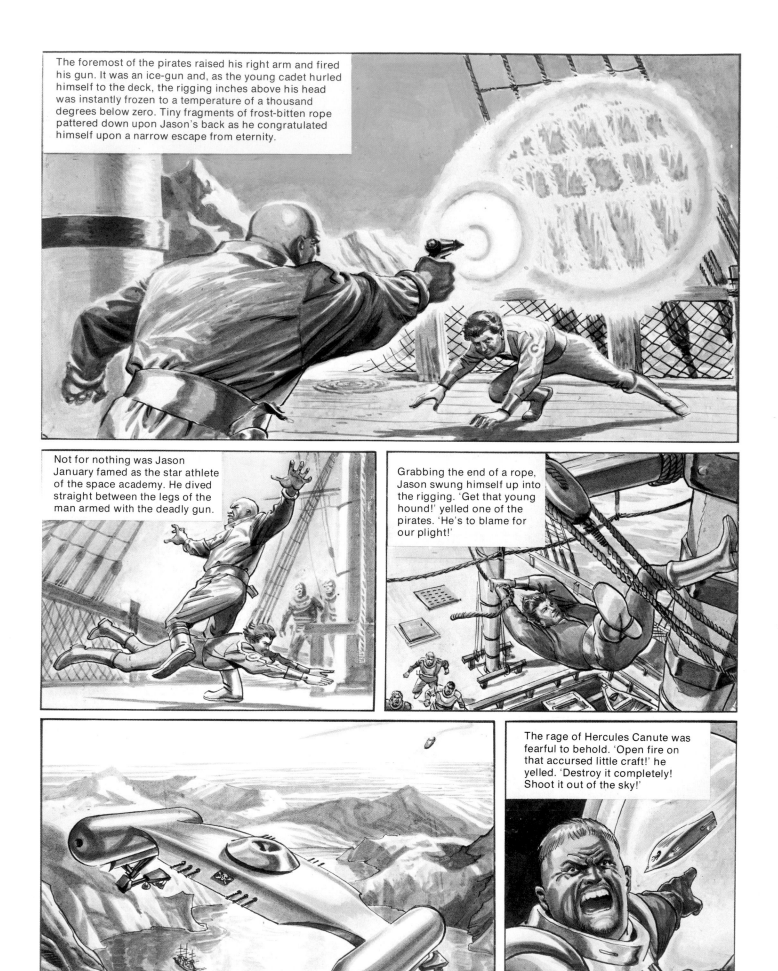

The foremost of the pirates raised his right arm and fired his gun. It was an ice-gun and, as the young cadet hurled himself to the deck, the rigging inches above his head was instantly frozen to a temperature of a thousand degrees below zero. Tiny fragments of frost-bitten rope pattered down upon Jason's back as he congratulated himself upon a narrow escape from eternity.

Not for nothing was Jason January famed as the star athlete of the space academy. He dived straight between the legs of the man armed with the deadly gun.

Grabbing the end of a rope, Jason swung himself up into the rigging. 'Get that young hound!' yelled one of the pirates. 'He's to blame for our plight!'

The rage of Hercules Canute was fearful to behold. 'Open fire on that accursed little craft!' he yelled. 'Destroy it completely! Shoot it out of the sky!'

The pirates' attempt to pick up the *Victory* with their grab had been foiled by the Rangers' space craft.

As the Rangers dived to the attack, a ripple of gunfire blazed from the bristling gun positions along the fuselage of the pirate craft. Miraculously, the Space Academy ship came through the peril, and opened fire on the enemy with its only armament . . . one single disintegrating cannon.

The cadets of the Ranger class yelled with delight to see the pirate ship turn and break off the action. 'We've got them on the run,' shouted one. 'We mustn't let them off the hook now. After them and bring them down!'

The Rangers' very first blast scored a devastating hit near the leading edge of the pirate craft, smashing the electrical systems of the gun positions.

At the end of the yard-arm, the young cadet raised himself gingerly to his feet. A sinking feeling gripped him in the pit of the stomach, as he stood poised for a breath-taking high dive into the water where the beasts awaited him.

But cadet Nick Ringold, in command, believed in first things first. 'Let them go,' he gritted. 'In due course, they can be sought out and destroyed. Our main task is to rescue Jason January . . . and to recover the *Victory* for Britain!'

Meanwhile, far below, Jason was in trouble. With the vengeful pirates on his heels, he had climbed out on a yard-arm . . . ready to jump and take a chance in the monster-filled lagoon!

Convinced that Jason would lack the resolve the make the death-defying plunge, the blood-thirsty convicts on the main-mast took careful aim with their weapons. 'I don't envy him his choice!' muttered one. 'He can be torn to pieces by those fiendish things in the lagoon or stay put on that yard-arm and be put permanently into deep freeze by our ice-guns! Since he can't seem to make up his mind, we'll make it up for him!'

Jason broke the surface of the water and the force of his dive sent him to the uttermost depths of the lagoon. Strange multi-coloured weeds and marine growths carpeted the rocky floor.

The moment the first convict triggered his ice-gun, Jason sprang from the yard-arm and hurtled downwards. The freezing blast from the gun missed him by mere inches.

Among a dense clump of weed, something stirred – something huge and menacing. It was yet another variety of the hideous monsters which had come into being on the Island of Wu-Cheng as a result of the atomic tests of the 20th century.

Fighting his way to the surface and gulping in a great mouthful of life-giving air, Jason beheld a huge pair of slavering jaws.

It seemed that nothing could save Jason from the beast! Then it happened! He heard the blast of powerful rocket engines.

He looked up and saw a rope ladder swaying down towards him. Jason's comrades had come to his rescue.

His hands reached up and grasped the ladder tight. The 'Ranger' craft rose swiftly, lifting Jason from the water and clear of the snapping jaws.

Jason swarmed up the rope-ladder into the space craft and clasped Nick Ringold by the hand. 'We got your S.O.S.,' said Nick. 'Now to recover the Victory.'

Nick and Jason were exchanging brief details of their adventures, when one of the crew raised a pointing finger. 'Look! Somebody is in big trouble down below on Wu-Cheng Island!' he shouted.

Hercules Canute had dropped six of his men in an armoured capsule to tackle the monsters. Now the gigantic brutes had dragged the capsule ashore and were tossing it about . . . with the pirates inside.

A touch on the controls brought the 'Ranger' craft hovering above the nightmare scene. Jason January rapped out an order. 'Fire a smoke shell!' he cried. 'It may scare the creatures!'

Wham! A shell from the cadet craft nose cannon burst on the coral beach, and instantly the monsters were engulfed in blinding, swirling smoke.

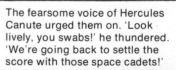

Again the rope ladder was dropped . . . and Jason and Nick swarmed down into the smoke to rescue the space pirates.

Meanwhile, a hundred miles up in the stratosphere, Canute's damaged craft was in orbit. Its crewmen were slaving to repair its hull.

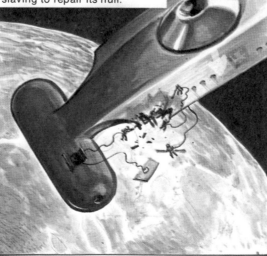

The fearsome voice of Hercules Canute urged them on. 'Look lively, you swabs!' he thundered. 'We're going back to settle the score with those space cadets!'

While the monsters stamped and blundered about, half-choked and completely blinded by the thick, lingering smoke, Jason and Nick dragged the terrified pirates from the battered remains of their armoured capsule. 'Come on, you rogues,' shouted Nick. 'It's more than you deserve, but we cannot stand by and watch men devoured by creatures such as inhabit this place!'

Urging the pirates ahead of them, Jason and Nick climbed up to their space craft, hovering in the sunlight above the smoke.

Guided by the cadets, the pirates seized the ladder with trembling hands and commenced to mount it.

Their escape seemed to have gone completely undetected by the monsters, and Jason heaved a sigh of relief as he clambered aboard. Then, through the hatch, he saw a talon.

Rearing high on its hind legs, one of the creatures had seized the space craft. Jason pressed the button which closed the door.

CLOSE

Inside the space craft, there was a scene of utter pandemonium as the deck tossed and heaved alarmingly. Keeping his head, Jason slammed the twin throttles open.

The atomic engines blasted to full power, and the 'Ranger' craft slowly clawed its laborious way skywards . . . lifting the enormous monster with it.

The engines faltered under the strain. 'If we can't shake that thing off, we'll crash into the lagoon' said Nick Ringold grimly.

Obedient to the controls, the space craft's nose rose vertically. The monster's roar of fury reached the ears of those inside the pressurised hull as its grasp slipped from the tapering sides of the ship. Down plunged the beast into the lagoon below.

Nick Ringold took over the controls and they circled over the lagoon in search of the *Victory*. 'There she is! She's drifted close to that small island!' cried Jason.

'Land the craft on the island,' said Jason. 'And keep a lookout for the pirates who were left aboard the *Victory*!'

The pirates had clambered on to the island. They glared in anger as they saw the Rangers' space craft descending.

One half-drew his ice-gun but another stayed his hand. 'It's no use,' he said. 'We're out-numbered!'

Jason was the first to set foot upon the ground. He sized up the situation at one glance. 'You villains had better surrender!' he declared. 'That is unless you want to stay here for ever.'

For a moment the pirates' decision was in the balance. Then one of them spoke up. 'But for these boys, we'd have been marooned here,' he growled. 'Hercules Canute has abandoned us. I say that we're finished with him and everything he stands for.'

'Help us to get the *Victory* back to Britain,' urged Jason. 'It will stand you in good stead at your trial.'

The pirates gazed up at the towering masts of Nelson's ancient ship . . . and then at the tiny Rangers' space craft. 'How do you think you can get her back?' asked one. 'That craft of yours couldn't lift the old hulk more than ten feet into the air.'

And then Jason dropped his bombshell. 'We're going to SAIL the *Victory* back,' he cried. 'Just like Admiral Nelson's tars did in days of yore!'

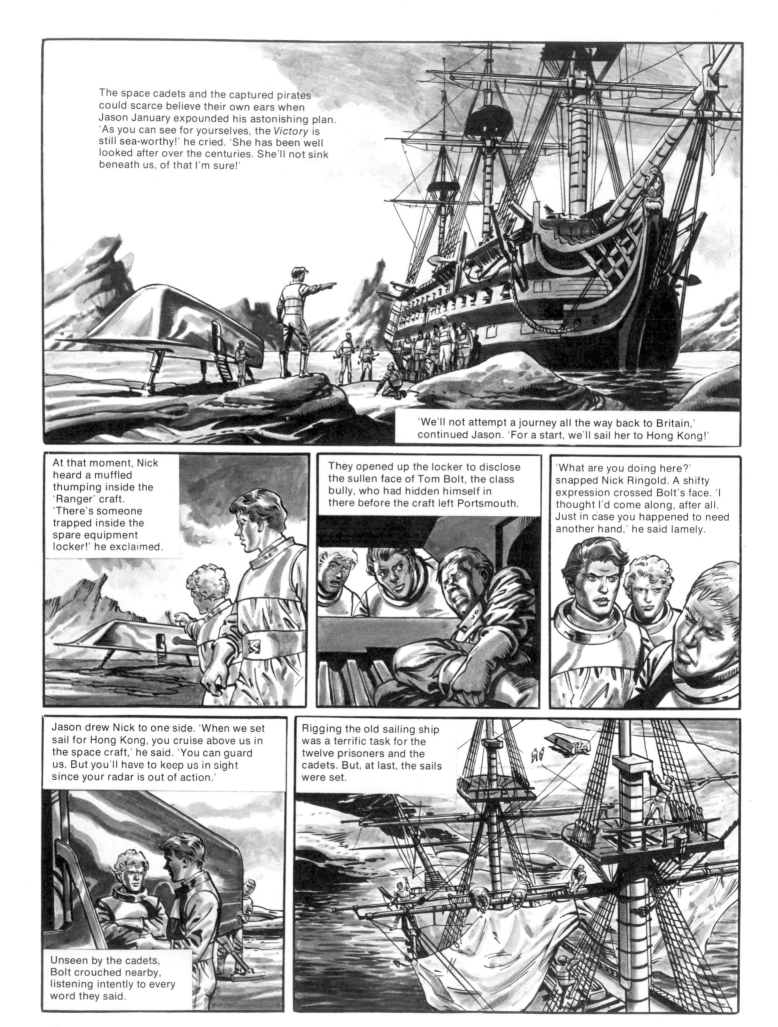

The space cadets and the captured pirates could scarce believe their own ears when Jason January expounded his astonishing plan. 'As you can see for yourselves, the *Victory* is still sea-worthy!' he cried. 'She has been well looked after over the centuries. She'll not sink beneath us, of that I'm sure!'

'We'll not attempt a journey all the way back to Britain,' continued Jason. 'For a start, we'll sail her to Hong Kong!'

At that moment, Nick heard a muffled thumping inside the 'Ranger' craft. 'There's someone trapped inside the spare equipment locker!' he exclaimed.

They opened up the locker to disclose the sullen face of Tom Bolt, the class bully, who had hidden himself in there before the craft left Portsmouth.

'What are you doing here?' snapped Nick Ringold. A shifty expression crossed Bolt's face. 'I thought I'd come along, after all. Just in case you happened to need another hand,' he said lamely.

Jason drew Nick to one side. 'When we set sail for Hong Kong, you cruise above us in the space craft,' he said. 'You can guard us. But you'll have to keep us in sight since your radar is out of action.'

Unseen by the cadets, Bolt crouched nearby, listening intently to every word they said.

Rigging the old sailing ship was a terrific task for the twelve prisoners and the cadets. But, at last, the sails were set.

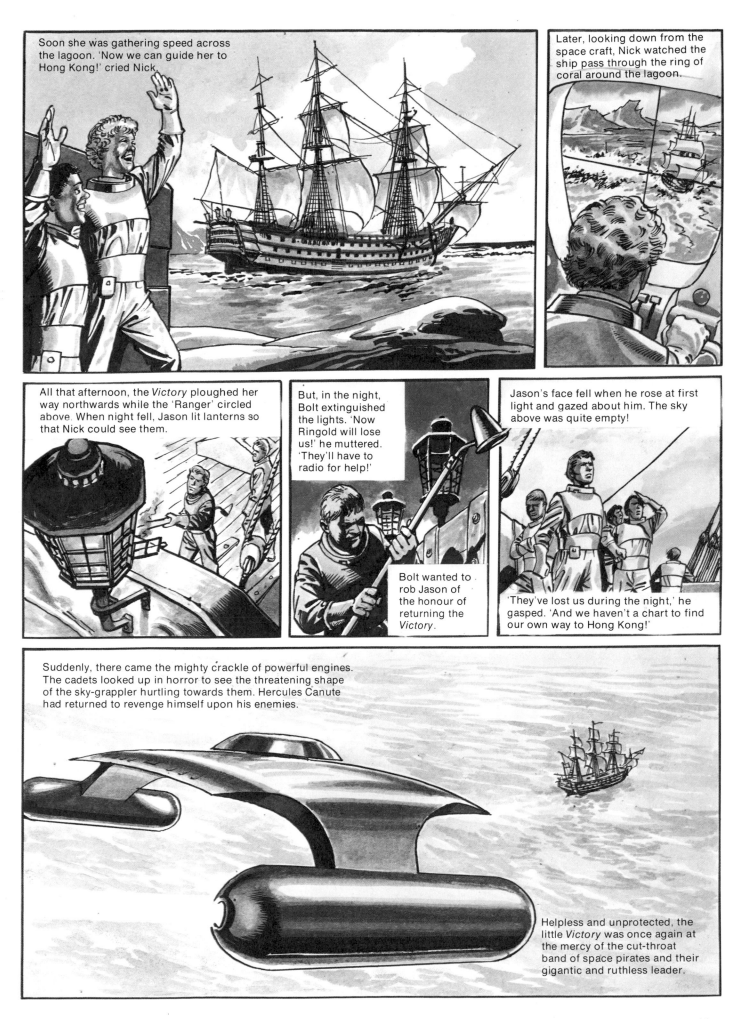

Soon she was gathering speed across the lagoon. 'Now we can guide her to Hong Kong!' cried Nick.

Later, looking down from the space craft, Nick watched the ship pass through the ring of coral around the lagoon.

All that afternoon, the *Victory* ploughed her way northwards while the 'Ranger' circled above. When night fell, Jason lit lanterns so that Nick could see them.

But, in the night, Bolt extinguished the lights. 'Now Ringold will lose us!' he muttered. 'They'll have to radio for help!'

Bolt wanted to rob Jason of the honour of returning the *Victory*.

Jason's face fell when he rose at first light and gazed about him. The sky above was quite empty!

'They've lost us during the night,' he gasped. 'And we haven't a chart to find our own way to Hong Kong!'

Suddenly, there came the mighty crackle of powerful engines. The cadets looked up in horror to see the threatening shape of the sky-grappler hurtling towards them. Hercules Canute had returned to revenge himself upon his enemies.

Helpless and unprotected, the little *Victory* was once again at the mercy of the cut-throat band of space pirates and their gigantic and ruthless leader.

Hercules Canute pressed his blunt and massive fore-finger on a control button, and the twin clamps with which his craft was fitted dropped from the pods which housed them. Like some mighty hawk swooping down upon its prey, the mighty space-grappler zoomed downwards towards the tiny *Victory*, where Jason and his comrades stood irresolute and helpless.

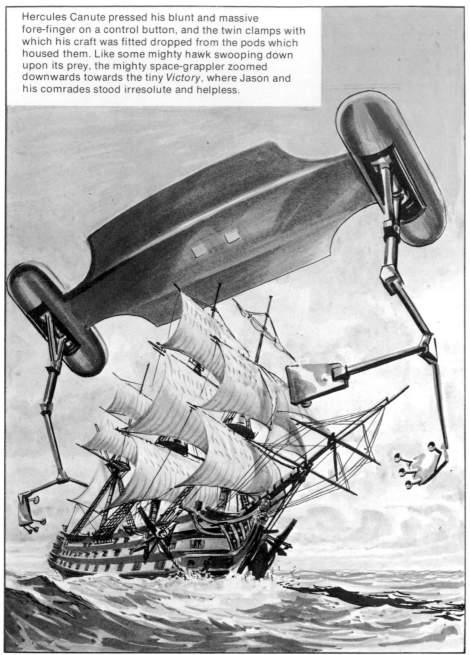

An evil grin twisted Canute's mouth as he gazed down at Jason. 'So the puny little pup thought he could thwart me!' he gloated. 'By the rings of Saturn, he shall learn his lesson!'

Jason could only stand and watch as the clamps came down to seize the hull.

The pirate prisoners the cadets had rescued were delighted by this unexpected turn of events. They decided it would be in their own interest to rejoin the force of Hercules Canute.

In a trice, the cowardly ex-prisoners turned upon the youths who had earlier saved their lives . . . and a desperate struggle followed.

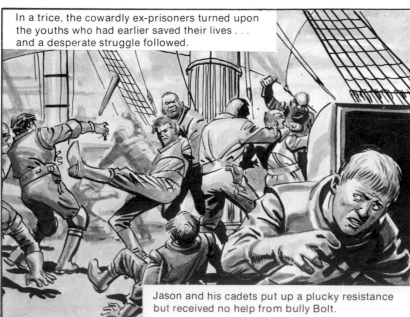

Jason and his cadets put up a plucky resistance but received no help from bully Bolt.

Soon the cadets were overcome and the pirates found Bolt cowering behind one of the guns. He was dragged to his feet.

And so the *Victory* was once again in the possession of Hercules Canute. Once Jason and his comrades had been overpowered, Nelson's flag-ship was lifted clear of the water by the incredibly powerful pirate craft.

A rope-ladder was lowered from a hatchway and dangled down past the towering main-mast to the deck of the *Victory*. Ice-guns were levelled menacingly and the cadets were ordered to make the dizzying climb up into the space craft.

Hercules Canute sat in his control chair like some ancient potentate upon a throne. 'You brats have caused me a lot of trouble!' he stormed. 'But now I have you and the *Victory* and you will be held to ransom for the return of my 200 imprisoned pirates!'

'Clap them in irons!' thundered Canute. Bolt's nerve broke. 'Not me,' he croaked. 'I helped you by putting out the ship's lights!'

Canute sent Bolt reeling with a contemptuous sweep of his hand. 'Set this swab to work in the galley!' he bellowed. 'Then lock the rest of 'em up!'

And so Jason and his lads were manacled and thrown into an empty compartment of the space ship. They sat glumly, pondering on their plight.

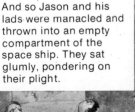

Hours later, the door opened, and a shame-faced Tom Bolt entered the compartment carrying a tray of bread and water for the cadets.

He was greeted angrily by his comrades. But Jason January silenced the outcry.

'I'm giving you a chance to redeem yourself, Bolt,' gritted Jason. 'You've got to steal the keys somehow and free us.'

The bully of the 'Ranger' class turned pale. 'Canute would kill me!' he faltered.

'Get the keys and release us, Bolt, or when we do eventually get free, we'll take you on one-by-one and give you the thrashing of your life!' grated Jason. 'That's a promise, Bolt. I warn you!' The remainder of the recruits murmured their agreement, and Bolt trembled.

'All right, chaps! I'll do what you say,' quavered Bolt. 'But I just hope you'll remember afterwards that I risked my life to save you!'

Reluctantly the cowardly bully crept into the vast control compartment where the keys hung in full view. He looked at the pirates intent upon their controls and licked his dry lips. How was he to seize the keys without being observed?

Suddenly the pirate operating the tele-radar cried out and pointed to his screen. 'Captain, there is an enemy craft approaching!' he shouted. Hercules Canute's beetling brow darkened with fury. 'It's that confounded cadet craft!' he roared at the top of his voice. 'Action stations!'

In the frantic activity that followed, no one saw Bolt snatch the keys and slip back into the compartment where his classmates awaited him. 'Well done, Bolt!' cried Jason. 'Unlock us!'

Seconds later, the Rangers' space craft was close enough to the pirates' ship to be discernible to the human eye as well as to the radar screen.

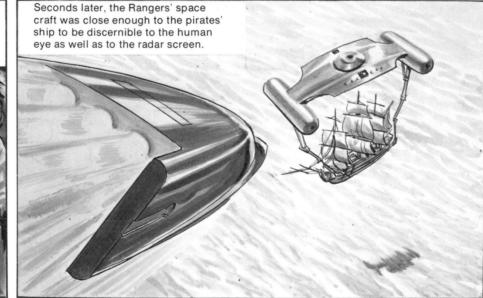

Nick and his comrades had been searching for the flag-ship. Their hearts sank when they realised that it was again in the clutches of Canute.

The pirates opened fire, and only the masterly handling of Nick Ringold at the controls saved the 'Ranger' class craft from complete destruction by the enemies' rockets.

They dared not return Canute's fire for fear of damaging the *Victory*. They also knew that their comrades might be on the pirate craft.

It was at that moment that Jason January and his companions crept into the control compartment of Hercules Canute's giant craft. One gunner was in the act of firing a nuclear bolt.

'At him, Rangers!' hissed Jason, and the cadets hurled themselves upon the unsuspecting gunner. The man never knew what had hit him. With a muffled groan, he slumped to the floor.

Jason seized the gun and swung it to face Hercules Canute and his astonished pirates. 'The game's up!' rasped Jason. 'You'd better surrender!'

The pirates were put in irons, and then Jason waved to the Ranger craft to let Nick Ringold know that everything was under control. 'Take over the space-grappler, lads!' he shouted. 'We'll take the old *Victory* back to England in style!'

And so, some time later, Nelson's ship was being lowered on to the base on which she had previously stood. Nick had radioed ahead, and a great welcome was awaiting.

But, while England rejoiced, strange events were taking place upon the planet Tarsen. The rulers of that planet were discussing a project to conquer the Earth.

The warlords of Tarsen decided that it would be foolish to invade until they knew the effectiveness of Earth's defences.

So three sturdy lads were called into the council chamber and given orders.

Their orders were to proceed as soon as possible to Earth, to pose as boys belonging to that planet and to get themselves enrolled at . . . the Royal Space Academy!

Continued on page 66

45

The Moon Camera

From the moment that eminent scientists concluded that a landing on the Moon could be made before the end of the century, vast amounts of money were allocated by the American and Russian governments to the venture.

Thereafter the scientists settled down to overcoming all the many difficulties and problems that barred the way. It was all very well to design space suits for the astronauts to wear and the craft that would rocket them to the Moon. Years were to pass while all these physical activities were carried out. Courageous men, such as the Russian Yuri Gagarin orbited Earth, as a preliminary step towards the ultimate goal of the Moon . . . and beyond.

But in order to prepare the way for astronauts to make their first real journey into the depths of space, as distinct from their merely orbiting their own planet, it was essential to discover as much as possible about the sort of conditions that they were likely to meet when they stepped out on to the Moon's surface.

The idea, as frequently postulated in schoolboys' magazines, of a dauntless scientist and his youthful companions stepping into a rocket ship in Central Park, New York and tranquilly setting off into outer space to make a landing on the Moon, with all the ensuing hair-raising adventures of civilizations strongly reminiscent of Ancient Roman times, complete with bloodthirsty games in a Moon-type Colosseum, was, of course, the stuff of which childhood dreams are made.

The truth was far more down to earth. The scientists knew how vital it was to learn as much as possible about what conditions the astronauts could expect when they finally landed on the Moon.

A preliminary step was to build rocket spacecraft which could be sent out across the immense distance that separated the Earth from the Moon.

These early unmanned craft were designed to pass close to the Moon's surface, taking photographs as they hurtled by and transmitting them back across space to Earth. In this way, much information was gained about the lunar surface and geography.

Later, another type of rocket carrying a television camera was aimed straight at the Moon. As it approached the lunar surface at something like 8,050 kilometres (5,000 miles) per hour, it began transmitting pictures. Its final photograph was taken a split second before it crashed to destruction.

Finally, in May 1966, the American space experts perfected a more sophisticated Moon camera – the Surveyor.

The Surveyor Spacecraft was despatched to the Moon where it soft-landed and took pictures of its immediate surroundings, some of them from as close as a few inches.

Delicate and complex electronic systems had to function reliably at speeds of up to 37,000 kilometres (23,000 miles) per hour and automatic radar devices had to measure accurately the distance between the spacecraft and the Moon's surface, so that powerful retro-rockets could be fired automatically to slow the craft down and set it gently on the ground.

Once on the Moon's surface, the Surveyor's solar panels (seen clearly on top of our illustrations) converted the sun's energy into electric power and used it to operate the television camera and radio transmitter.

Surveyor robot spacecraft sent back scores of thousands of pictures of the Moon, together with other information about conditions such as temperatures and even the composition of soil and rocks in their immediate vicinity. The supreme value of all this study and costly experimentation was justified when a man stepped down a ladder and trod the surface of the Moon for the first time.

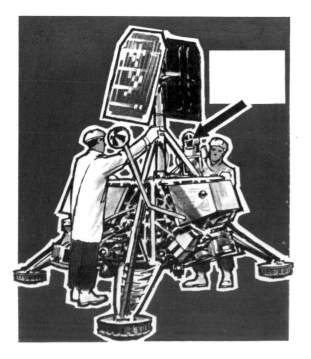

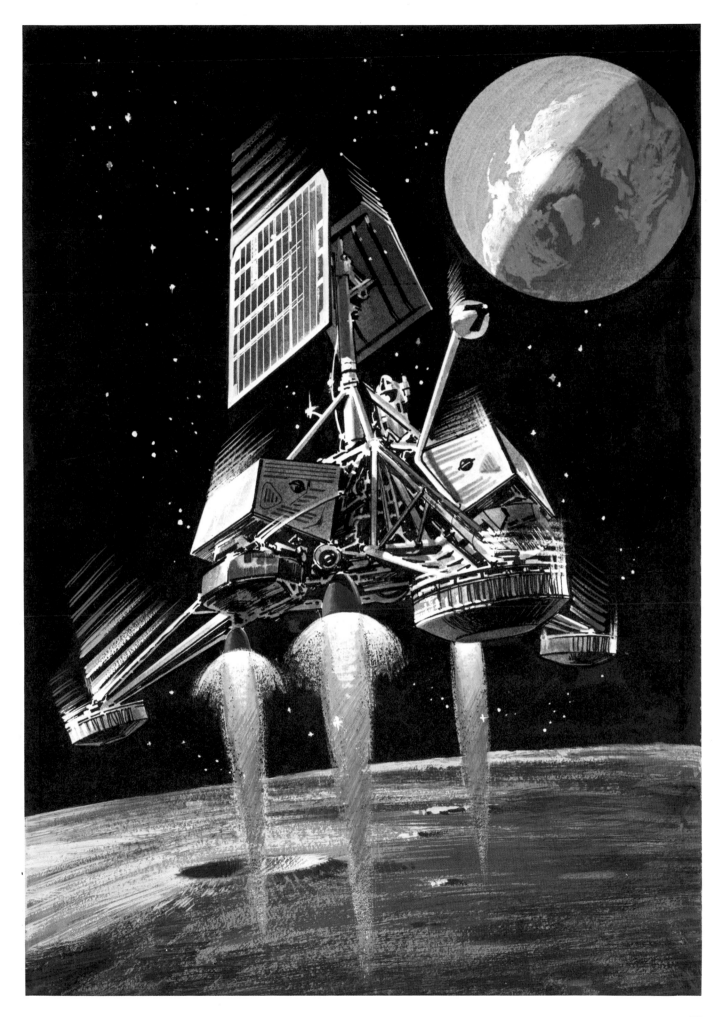

47

Great Balls
of Fire

'Prepare for earth-atmosphere re-entry,' crisply orders the commander of the returning space shuttle.

The scientists returning to Earth after a spell of duty in an orbiting space laboratory look at each other anxiously and prepare themselves for the tremendous pull of the Earth's gravity on their tiny ship.

Even more frightening is the fact that as their shuttle hurtles at an incredibly fast speed into the mixture of gases that surround the Earth, the exterior skin of their shuttle will become a ball of fire, more intensely hot than the hottest surface.

Officials at the North America Space Administration headquarters are tracking the shuttle on their radar screens. A mass of technical information from the shuttle is fed to a myriad of dials. The one that attracts a lot of attention is a temperature indicator.

It shows how hot it is on the skin of the craft and how hot it is inside, where, if the thermal protection fails, the scientists may be roasted alive.

But the NASA officials are pinning their faith on a coating of heat-resistant tiles that covers the outer casing of the shuttle. As the shuttle races through the air, the friction between it and the atmosphere creates the incredibly intense heat that the scientists have anticipated. However, inside the shuttle the passengers feel warm but not uncomfortably so. And when their shuttle lands like a conventional plane, they step out, glad to be home and physically unharmed by the experience they have been through.

Amazing? Incredible? Of course! But scenes like this could become commonplace in years to come.

The problem has been to provide the shuttle with a protective skin that can stand up to a hundred re-entries without failing.

After many experiments, America's Lockheed company has made some tiles which could be fastened to the exterior of the shuttle. They are designed to lose their surface heat very rapidly so that they do not convey it, by conduction, to the shuttle's shell. These tiles can withstand repeated heating and cooling without damage.

They can be taken white hot from a kiln and plunged into cold water without coming to harm. And it is possible to hold one with the bare fingers without injury while it is still glowing white hot after being heated in an oven.

The basic raw material for the tiles is sand from which are made the silica fibres that compose the tiles. A cement containing the fibres is mixed with water and a binder and cast into soft, porous blocks. Tiles are cut from these blocks, coated with a silica mixture and then baked in an oven.

Tiles for the underside of the shuttle receive a glass coating that is able to resist very high

temperatures without being damaged.

The tiles intended for the upper surfaces have a white shiny surface intended to reflect the sun's rays and keep the shuttle cool while in orbit.

A water-proofing compound is added to prevent the tiles from absorbing extra weight in rain or humidity. Cutting tiles to fit the complex shape of a shuttle is so complicated that no two tiles are alike. Computer-controlled milling machines are used to cut them. Fitting them on to the space craft will be as tricky as assembling a jigsaw puzzle more than twice the size of a tennis court.

Further to complicate matters, the small gaps between the tiles – from where air trapped by the tiles is allowed to escape to prevent expansion – must be uniform to within a very small margin. Nearly 34,000 tiles are needed to cover about 70% of the aircraft's surface. An arduous task indeed.

Experiments, experiments, experiments. That sums up the life of the average space scientist. Does it sound dull? The scientists do not think so. To them, this type of work is the most important on Earth and so long as there is limitless space to be explored, the work of the space scientist will continue.

Games of Peril

On the planet Arvan the silence of the velvety night was suddenly shattered by the roar of an approaching spacecraft, and a few moments later a Courier Space-jet alighted gracefully in a clearing of short-cut purple grass. A door slid open and three Earthmen and an attractive red-haired Earthwoman stepped out and descended the short metal ladder leading to the ground.

The young woman, who emerged first, was followed by a tall, gloomy looking man in immaculate Spacefleet uniform, a wiry little Space engineer and a thick-set flaxen-haired Army lieutenant.

The four were, in fact, an ace group of secret operatives from Earth, agents with a long string of successful operations behind them. During the course of their activities they had made many grateful friends . . . and many more ruthless enemies.

They were now en route to a meeting that had been called by Sir John Grainger, Earth Ambassador to Arvan. They had not been informed of the reason for the summons, this because of the total secrecy requested by Grainger. That there must be something seriously worrying the Ambassador was, however, obvious, for he would never have sent for the four agents unless the situation demanded their immediate and exclusive presence.

All four headed towards a splendid building constructed of Arvan marble that gleamed softly in the gentle radiance of the night.

'I wonder . . .' began Ben Hogan, the stocky Army man, when suddenly the ground beneath his feet seemed to give way. All four agents were suddenly launched into space to drop with brain-numbing swiftness to the depths below.

Down, down, down fell the four comrades, senses reeling but all aware that their mission had met with an early disaster, if not conclusion.

All were astonished to land on a carpet of sponge-like material that effectively broke their fall without breaking their bones.

Rex Blane, Space Commander, staggered to his feet, eyes blinking, hands to whirling head.

'What in the name of all that's . . .' he winced. That was as far as he got for a mocking sibilant voice interrupted him.

'Welcome, thrice welcome to you and your gallant companions, Commander Blane. I will endeavour to make your short stay on Arvan as entertaining as possible.'

Rex looked about him for a loud-speaker but without success. The voice, harsh and rendered discordant and unrecognizable by some quirk in the transmitter, had seemed to come from no point in particular.

Before Rex could say anything, that sneering voice continued.

'I regret that for the moment we cannot enjoy a lengthy conversation, Commander, but you see, for the last few moments you and your friends have been inhaling a certain sleep-inducing gas. Ever heard of Pestamytholone?'

Rex stared blearily at his three fellow-agents. All lay unconscious.

'Hee, hee, hee,' cackled the weird voice. 'Your friends are obviously more susceptible to the gas than you are, Commander. Even so, I venture to believe that you can feel your senses slipping away . . . but have no fear. I do not intend that you will die at my hands . . . *yet!*'

But Rex Blane was no longer listening. He was already a crumpled heap beside his senseless friends.

A full minute passed and then from behind a towering tree nearby there stepped the owner of the mysterious voice. An ugly smile disfigured his strange features.

'So!' he muttered. 'Space Commander Blane, Space Engineer Jim Love, Lieutenant Ben Hogan and Doctor Jill Mandrake! My old enemies from planet Earth – here for a last reckoning. Well, Mr Ambassador Grainger will have to wait in vain tonight for the arrival of Earth's most efficient action-group.'

While he was speaking, a squad of well-drilled figures had been moving stealthily out of the surrounding forest.

Their mysterious leader chuckled amusedly as the unconscious Earth agents were lifted and taken away by his henchmen.

'To think that the high-and-mighty top-echelon agent of Earth and his oh-so-clever friends should all have walked into a simple pit-fall . . . the sort of trap that was laid by their ancestors when hunting tigers in the jungles of India. How laughable! I must see that they rue their unwonted stupidity.'

He laughed aloud and then broke into uncontrollable merriment as he heard the engines of the Courier Space-jet that had brought Rex Blane and his companions from Earth roar into life. The spacecraft sped away into the sky, its crew completely oblivious of the fate that had so suddenly overtaken their erstwhile passengers.

* * *

Rex Blane winced as he opened his eyes for a brief moment. His whole head ached intolerably and the back of his throat seemed to be on fire. He groaned and opening his eyes for a second time, looked about him.

He was sprawled, twisted uncomfortably, in a low chair on a patio outside a small hut that seemed to be made entirely of metal. Its sides gleamed in the early morning sun. Rex realised that he had been unconscious all night.

'Rex!' The voice came from behind him. He sat up and turned round, trying not to succumb to the pain that immediately ripped through his head.

Ben Hogan was getting to his feet, rubbing his head as he did so.

'Thank the stars you're awake, chum,' he said stumblingly. 'I thought you were all dead.'

Weavingly he went over to Doctor Jill Mandrake, the attractive red-headed young woman who was one of Earth's top nuclear scientists.

'How's it going, Doc?' he asked gently.

'Terrible!' the girl groaned. 'I don't know how or why but we've been gassed! Pestamytholone, I'd say. One of the strongest nerve-gases ever invented.'

Rex managed to summon up a grin.

'You don't know how right you are, Jill,' he said. Then he looked round as he heard Jim Love's voice.

'Could you try to speak in a whisper, Commander? My head's splitting.'

'Apart from that?' Rex wanted to know.

'Okay,' replied the little Space Engineer.

'Right. Then let's see where we go from here,' said Rex, levering himself out of the chair and getting uncertainly to his feet.

'You're not going very far, Commander Blane,' broke in the harsh unrecognizable voice that Rex had heard the night before. 'That is not to say, however, that I do not want you and your three companions to try. Oh yes. You must try to escape my clutches for that is the whole purpose of the exercise.'

'Hey!' exclaimed Jim. 'Who's that?'

'And what's your game?' demanded Ben.

The Voice answered: '"Game" is the operative word, Commander Blane. Your companion Hogan is to be commended on his happy choice of word. Yes, game – for you are all here to take part in a few little games of my own devising. Your antics will, I truly believe, provide me with much amusement.'

The sinister voice dropped to a lower pitch. 'I have set you a number of tasks which you must perform. If you are successful you may leave this place freely and of your own accord. But if you fail . . . then you will all die.'

'What utter nonsense,' said Rex Blane in a matter-of-fact voice.

'You think so?' asked the equable voice. 'You will not have long to wait.' There followed a long silence while the four agents stared at each other.

'What in the name of Heaven . . .' began Jim Love when, before he could utter another word, the little group heard the sound of drumming feet, a growing thunder that as it grew nearer shook the very ground beneath them. Then suddenly out of the vivid scarlet trees nearby there crashed a huge Hebragryff, a monstrous Arvanian animal that resembled the prehistoric-Earth triceratops, scales and heavy armour and all – save that the Hebragryff was far more vicious.

'Make for cover!' yelled Rex, tearing from his belt a Spacefleet regulation blaster, a hand-gun that could cut a man in half at full power. In response to his bellow, Jill Mandrake, Ben Hogan and Jim Love fled for shelter behind the steel hut. As the mighty Hebragryff bore down on him, Rex dodged swiftly to one side. As he did so, his finger involuntarily squeezed the blaster's trigger and the frightful energy bolt erupt-

ing from the gun shot straight down the gaping jaws of the beast. Blood spurted in great streams and the Hebragryff halted in mid-stride, its lowered head weaving slowly from side to side, a scarlet river flooding from its spasmodically twitching lips. Rex could only watch in silence. Then slowly, oh so slowly, the monster sank to its knees, let loose a horrible bubbling scream and toppled over on to its side, its huge legs kicking in death throes. One last gasp and it was dead, but if Rex was relieved by its demise he was in for another shock for two more Hebragryffs suddenly crashed upon the scene and made straight for him.

'Quick, Rex!' came Ben Hogan's voice behind him. 'In here!'

Whirling, Rex saw Ben, Jim and Jill standing at the open door of the small steel hut. Without more ado, he turned and dashed towards them with the Hebragryffs in hot pursuit. As he streaked into the hut, Ben Hogan slammed the door behind him and as Rex slithered to a halt he heard the mighty animals thundering past the hut.

'Phew! that was close,' gasped Rex, wiping his forearm across his perspiring forehead.

'Games the man said,' said Jim Love, tight-lipped. 'Not exactly the sort of games I used to play at nursery school.'

'Who's surprised?' chimed in Ben Hogan. 'What sort of game was it that hoodwinked us into walking over the edge of a cliff last night? The ground between us and the Embassy seemed firm enough when we started to walk towards it. How come we walked over the edge of a ravine?'

'A pitfall,' explained Doctor Jill Mandrake. 'We didn't see the pitfall ahead of us because whoever is responsible for all this fun-and-games used some devilish form of auto-suggestion that created in the minds of all of us the mirage of firm ground ahead of us.'

'Brilliant!' interrupted that hated voice of mockery. 'It is clear that nuclear research is not the only science in which you excel, Doctor.'

'There's that man again,' said Jim Love.

'Ready for the next round of fun?' asked the voice, emanating once again from some hidden loud-speaker. 'Look about you. What do you see?'

Dutifully the four agents stared round the room. It was completely bare of furniture and ornamentation, while walls, ceiling and floor appeared to be made of steel. There was only one door. Quickly Rex stepped across to it and strove to open it. The door was securely locked. The voice laughed.

'No, no, Commander Blane. That door is securely locked and as you can see, there is no keyhole on your side of the door. It can only be opened from the outside – as Lieutenant Hogan opened it just now so that you could all rush inside and escape the Hebragryffs. Ha, ha! You must admit that my little games are well planned.'

'And so?' barked Rex.

'And so you must get out of the room in which you are now imprisoned. But – and it is a big "but" – you must escape within a certain time.'

'And why?'

'Because all the air is being slowly extracted from the room and if you do not get out fast, you will all soon suffocate. Goodbye for now!'

Rex glanced grimly at his friends.

'Right! You heard the man – let's go!' he said and swiftly the four of them ranged around the walls, feeling for the tiniest crack that would indicate a doorway. But there was none. The steel walls were smooth and shiny and it seemed as though the room had been constructed from one long strip of metal. Even the floor was solid all the way round.

'It's no use,' grunted Jim Love. 'We're well and truly trapped. Darn it, it's getting difficult to breathe already,' and he loosened his collar.

Savagely he smashed a foot against the nearest wall. But all to no avail. The sound of the blow echoed around the room.

Rex felt as though a weight was pressing down on his chest. Beads of perspiration stood out on his brow and trickled into his eyes.

'We've got to think!' he mumbled. 'Wait!' He stiffened as an idea came to him. 'Of course – the ceiling! Jim, climb on to Ben's shoulders. See what the ceiling's made of!'

The wiry little Space Engineer clambered on to Ben Hogan's broad shoulders and put a hand up to the ceiling. Whereupon he exclaimed aloud.

'Why, it's not steel at all up here, Commander. It's some sort of fibre, painted to look like steel!'

'Then smash through it if you can,' growled Ben Hogan. 'You're a heck of a weight to carry when I'm struggling for my next breath, Jim.'

Clenching his fist, Jim Love struck a heavy blow at the ceiling – and his hand went straight through it.

'Why, it's like paper,' he gasped. 'It's porous – lets air through, anyway. How come we've been suffocating?'

'More auto-suggestion,' smiled Doctor Jill.

Rex frowned. 'You mean that voice suggested that we might suffocate and so we began to feel that we were – even though we weren't? Yes, you could be right at that, Jill. The closed-in atmosphere of the steel walls would help the illusion along. Why, that fiend. . . .'

Suddenly, as if by magic, one of the walls of the little room fell away and the sinister voice sounded again.

'A fiend? No, a genius, Commander. Now then, let me see how well you can distinguish reality from fantasy in your next task which is, quite simply, to walk from where you are to the tree you see in front of you.'

The four friends peered through the gap and saw that they were looking through the back of the hut. The little steel room seemed to be situated on a high cliff overlooking a vast valley covered by thick jungle, through which a river meandered lazily.

All round the room the ground was covered with rows of curious bright red, frondlike plants, about six inches high.

At the very edge of the cliff stood a tall tree, the bark of which was silver and the leaves of a coppery colour.

'It all looks too easy,' murmured Rex. 'But let's go and keep our eyes open.'

He stepped across the rows of fronds towards the lone tree. But as he did so, one of the fronds gripped his ankle and another whipped up his leg to his knee and curled round, tripping him up so that he fell heavily to the ground. He strove to free himself but it was useless. The fronds were gripping him with a strength that was almost unbelievable.

'Arvanian man-traps!' cried Doctor Jill, holding back Ben and Jim. 'They cover you, strangle you with their fronds and then suckers at their roots slowly extract your blood as you lie there.'

By now Rex was struggling desperately.

'How can we save the Commander, Jill?' asked Ben, his voice breaking anxiously.

Rex heard Jill's reply dimly penetrating his consciousness.

'Don't struggle, whatever you do! Grip the roots of the plants and pull them from the earth. It's your only chance!'

With a last effort, Rex twisted on to his side and gripped the frond that was lashed round his right hand by the root. With a swift, sharp tug he pulled the root out completely.

A half-human squeal rang piercingly through the air. The frond loosened its grip on his hand and fell away – a dead plant!

'You're a clever little girl, Doctor,' came the evil voice menacingly, as freeing himself of the rest of the sinuous plants, Rex floundered back into the steel hut. 'But now I am beginning to lose my patience.' As the voice died away, the floor beneath the feet of the four friends suddenly trembled and then swiftly descended, carrying them down to a vast shining room. There a body of grimly scowling Arvanian guards armed with blaster-ray rifles was awaiting them. Hovering high above them was a creature that all four Earth agents remembered well . . . only too well in fact.

'By Jupiter!' breathed Rex. 'Karnak!'

Grotesquely ugly beyond imagination, Karnak leered down at them and his shrill screaming voice resounded throughout the chamber.

'Yes, I, Karnak!' he shrieked. 'Many times, Blane, you have defeated me but this time – aha, this time *you* can taste the bitter dregs of defeat. Was it not an English poet who centuries ago wrote "What though the field be lost? All is not lost. Th'unconquerable will, and study, revenge"? Well, long have I studied my revenge and now at last it is at hand.'

While Karnak had been viciously spewing his hatred, Rex had been looking round the huge room. Weird, intricate machinery whirred softly on all sides and in the middle of the floor was a large glass dome through which could be seen gleaming power circuits and crystal energy rods that stabbed ceaselessly forwards and backwards.

Expressionlessly, Rex stared up at Karnak, swooping to and fro, still mouthing his hatred in a string of oaths and foul curses. Possessor of many powers, one of which was the ability to defy gravity, he was the dictator-in-exile of Arvan, with a fiendishly cunning and power-crazed brain whose only thought was complete conquest of the entire Galaxy. Long had he been believed dead but Rex realised that Sir John Grainger, the Earth Ambassador, had learned somehow that Karnak was alive and loose and had sent for him and his three daring friends to tackle the dire problem of putting an end to the mad dictator once and for all.

'You will always be a threat to me, Blane,' Karnak was raging, 'and so you must die. Guards – dispose of them!'

It was at this moment that Rex suddenly whipped out his regulation blaster, that same gun that had slain the Hebragryff, and before one startled guard could pull a trigger, he had aimed it at the power-dome – the only place, he suspected, that would create enough damage to give them a chance of survival – and fired.

A blaster-bolt exploded in the centre of the dome, completely destroying the glass covering and wrecking the hissing pistons and delicate machinery within. Came a violent blinding flash and a deafening explosion, the roof of the great room shook and cracked across and chunks of fibre and concrete crashed to the floor.

'Down!' yelled Rex, clawing at Jill and dragging her to the floor. 'Down – all of you!' Jim Love and Ben Hogan dropped to the floor beside Rex and Jill as fire swept across the debris-strewn floor, engulfing the screaming Arvanian guards. A thick cloud of dust hid the dreadful scene from the group spread-eagled on the floor.

Then the noise ceased and the only sound to be heard was the crackle of flames from the burning wreckage.

'Phew!' gasped Rex, getting to his feet. 'Looks like the end of Karnak for I saw him blown to smithereens by the explosion.'

Circuits had been shorted by the tremendous explosion. This was the cause of the roaring fire that now enveloped the major part of the huge chamber.

Dead and dying Arvanian guards littered the floor. Doctor Jill Mandrake stared open-eyed at several writhing forms, tears of sympathy streaming down her cheeks.

'Can't we do something to help those poor souls?' she asked, but Rex shook his head. He was once again the cool Space Commander, careful in this emergency only for the welfare of his own companions.

'We've got to find our way out of here,' he said. 'After all, what do we know of this place? There may be scores of other Arvanians loyal to Karnak garrisoning the building. No, Jill. We must go – now!'

But Rex's fears were groundless. Karnak's villainies in the past had been so vicious and cruel that few men had rallied to his newly-raised banner. Those few had been the band of guards in the room that was now a raging holocaust of flames.

It did not take the four adventurers long to discover the way out of Karnak's hide-out. As they stepped out into the open air, Ben Hogan gave a sigh of relief.

'Never thought I'd see that blue sky again,' he grinned, 'especially when those tykes raised their rifles. That was quick thinking of you, Rex.'

'Yeah,' chuckled Jim Love, 'Talk about quick on the draw. Why, those old-time gunmen of the American West had nothing on you when it comes to quick shooting, Commander.'

Rex laughed. 'Come on. Let's go report to Sir John Grainger. He'll be wondering where we have got to.'

Under Pressure

Early on 22 February 1935, one of the world's most famous aircraft pilots, Wiley Post, took off from Burbank, California, in his equally famous plane, the Lockheed Vega *Winnie Mae*. Post had made the headlines for years in his astonishing career and he was about to do so again. This time he was flying to New York via the stratosphere, wearing the world's first practical pressure suit, which he had developed with much patience and help.

But all famous men have enemies and one of Post's had emptied a bag of abrasive emery dust into *Winnie Mae*'s engine. After half an hour, it began to splutter and throw oil down the fuselage so Post prepared for an emergency landing. As the engine cut out, he glided down towards the vast, white expanse of the Muroc, a dry lake bed in the Mojave desert in the South-western United States.

With the propeller set horizontal to avoid damage, Post put the plane, still heavy with fuel, down on its belly, skid aiming for a gentle feather-like touch-down. (This was normal; the aircraft had been fitted with an undercarriage which was dropped after take-off to save weight.)

A few hundred yards away, the owner of the local store was enjoying preparing a land-yacht built on to a car chassis. He did not hear Post's landing and nearly died of fright when Post suddenly appeared at his shoulder to ask for help in taking off the helmet of the cumbersome suit.

Wiley Post was a true pioneer, famous for the white eye-patch that covered an eye lost after an oil-rig accident in 1926. Among his exploits, still unique today, was his 1933 solo round-the-world flight made in seven days, eighteen hours and fifty minutes.

He had always been interested in flying high and was sparked into action by the announcement of an England-to-Australia air race to celebrate the hundredth year of the City of Melbourne. Sir Macpherson Robertson was offering a prize of £10,000 and a gold cup for the winner. Post decided he could take the prize despite the higher speeds of some aircraft newer than the ageing *Winnie Mae* if he was able to take her into the thin air above 9,144 metres (30,000 feet) and ride the incredibly powerful winds that he knew were there. (Post predicted the existence of these winds called 'jet streams' long before any pilot experienced them.)

He kept the idea a close secret, discussed it only with a few aviation friends and on 6 April 1934 he contacted the B.F. Goodrich Company in Los Angeles with the plan. He said he would

like a rubber suit which would enable him to survive the deadly low pressure in the stratosphere by cocooning him in pressurized oxygen to give a pressure on his body equivalent to 1,676 metres (5,500 feet).

The first crude suit and its knight-in-armour metal helmet with a slit for vision did not stand up to testing – it split under pressure. The second version was ruined when Post had to be cut out of it after putting on some weight between the first 'fittings' and the tests!

A third, much more advanced suit was now designed together with a second helmet, but testing was vital and *Winnie Mae* herself needed much modification with new equipment for high-altitude flight.

All this work eventually put Post out of the England-to-Australia race. However, he went on to prove the world's first practical pressure suit and so paved the way for the future space-flight and the eventual moon landing.

Throughout the remainder of 1934–35, Post made a number of pressure-suited flights, unheeding the danger in going so far into the unknown areas high above America. He reached 14,630 metres (48,000 feet) and also found the mighty jet-streams he had predicted.

Before the outbreak of World War II, yet another suit made news – this time a British design used by the pilots of the Bristol 138, an all-wooden monoplane with massive wings, designed for high-altitude flying. (As shown on the opposite page.)

In September 1936, Squadron Leader F.R.D. Swain took the planc to 15,230 metres (49,967 feet). Then in May 1937, an Italian pilot, Colonel M. Pezzi, took the record and on the last day of May, Flight Lieutenant M.J. Adam donned the suit and flew the Bristol 138 to a record 16,440 metres (53,937 feet). Only one incident marred the two and a quarter hour's flight. At about 15,240 metres (50,000 feet), Adam heard a sharp crack and found, to his relief that the only damage was a cracked pane in the cockpit roof, caused by contraction in the intense cold.

These early suits were limited in their effectiveness. The British suit (opposite page) would allow the wearer to remain at a height of 15,240 metres (50,000 feet) for a scant two hours. But valuable lessons were being learnt for the future.

A Boeing B-29 lumbered into the dawn sky at Edwards Air Force Base in the Mojave Desert of California, U.S.A. on 25 August 1949, clutching under its fuselage a tiny rocket plane, the Bell X-1 which, almost two years before, had been flown through the then unknown sound barrier for the first time.

Colonel Frank 'Pete' Everest, on his seventh X-1 flight, was attempting to reach 22,250 metres (73,000 fcct). At a mere 2,133 metres (7,000 feet), he lowered himself down on a miniature lift to the level of the X-1 cockpit door and squeezed inside. As he did so, he noticed a minute crack in one of the wind-screen panels but did not consider it bad enough to stop the flight.

Strapping himself in, Everest cursed the tight-laced pressure suit and its constricting helmet that in just a few minute's time he would bless for saving his life.

The B-29 pilot's countdown reached zero, the X-1 dropped, Everest flicked three of its rockets into life and soared steeply upwards. His craft went supersonic and leaped on into the dark sky. Then at 19,812 metres (65,000 feet) – a loud bang – and with an explosive hiss, the canopy split wide open and his air pressure vanished. The suit inflated immediately and clamped down on his whole body, like a giant vice.

With an enormous effort, he cut the rockets off and, fighting the suit, pushed the plane over into a steep dive for survival altitude. At 6,096 metres (20,000 feet) Everest was able to 'dump' the suit pressure and it relaxed its boa constrictor grip. He was alive, though badly shaken and able to guide his little orange plane down to a safe landing.

Everest owed his life to the T-1 partial-pressure suit, which was later worn by thousands of test pilots and military crews whose jobs took them to high altitudes.

* * *

What would have happened if he had not been wearing the suit?

A whole catalogue of horrors, depending on the altitude at which he had been exposed to low pressure, would have resulted.

A man can survive but the higher he goes, the less time he has. At 7,925 metres (26,000 feet), oxygen starvation begins in about two minutes, unconsciousness comes in three minutes. At 14,020 metres (46,000 feet), unconsciousness lasts eleven to twenty seconds, and above this level, oxygen can no longer enter the lungs even if it exists in the surrounding atmosphere.

The low pressure allows the waste-products of breathing (carbon dioxide and water-vapour) to fill the lungs. At 19,202 metres (63,000 feet), air pressure is so low that liquids will boil into vapour at 37°C (98°F), the average human body temperature – so blood will froth into vapour and cripple or kill the unprotected human being.

The protection against these and many other problems was painstakingly developed by aero-medical scientists and engineers who used themselves, dogs and monkeys to test their equipment. One scientist, clad in a primitive partial-pressure suit, put himself into a test chamber. At a pressure equalling 17,678 metres (58,000 feet), he watched in horror as his hands swelled up like balloons. The sweat on his palms and the heat generated in the low pressure had caused the nitrogen in his skin tissue to expand. He was soon 'brought down' or 'deflated' to ground level and quickly recovered.

Keeping pressure on the pilot's body was solved by squeezing him into a tight-laced suit fitted with inflatable tubes along the arms and legs. In emergencies, a pressure-sensing valve flooded the tubes with oxygen and they clamped the suit down hard. A tight helmet sealed to the suit at the neck completed the protection. The breathing problem was solved by a technique called 'reserve breathing'. Instead of sucking air in, the pilot had high-pressure oxygen forced into his lungs and he had to block it off at his nose and mouth, then force it out, and then allow the next 'breath' in, and so on.

Just as a mediaeval knight had to get used to fighting in clumsy armour, so the pressure-suited high-altitude pilot had to get used to the constricting grip of his suit and helmet and the reverse-breathing technique and still manage the delicate job of flying his high-speed touchy aircraft with precision!

*   *   *

In the mid-1950s, a different research aircraft progressed on the drawing boards of the North American (now Rockwell International) Aviation Co. It was code-named X-15 by the US Air Force and was to fly to undreamed-of heights at incredible speeds. It had two separate control systems, one for use in the atmosphere like other aircraft and a second using small gas jets for control on the edge of space where wings and tail would not 'bite.' Obviously the spaceman-pilots who would fly it could not do so in a device like the T-1 suit, developed with skill but little money.

The X-15 project pilot, Scott Crossfield, set about equipping himself with something adequate to the task and found the answer at the David C. Clark Company whose experts devised a new fine mesh link-net material which would be strong but flexible enough to allow the pilot freedom of movement under pressure. The link-net material covered a rubberized pressure

garment and was itself inside a silvered outer layer to protect against high temperatures, for the suit had also to be part of the escape system and might have to be used under all sorts of temperatures.

The whole thing was topped off by a recognisable 'space helmet' and was the first full-pressure 'space suit'. Wearing it, several pilots gained astronaut wings for flying the X-15 to a height above 80 kilometres (50 miles) from the earth's surface. In the course of 199 flights, from 1959 to 1967, three X-15s carried out much experimental work into unknown areas of air and space science. The maximum height reached was 108 kilometres (67 miles), the maximum speed 7,296 kilometres (4,534 miles) per hour. One of the pilots was a certain Neil Armstrong, of whom you may have heard.

Many of the experiments were connected with the manned space flights to come in the Mercury and Gemini series and the Clark full-pressure suit design was to go deeper into space!

It was 'all happening' in the space suit business in the early months of 1961. On April 12, Flight Major Yuri Gagarin blasted into the history books in his Vostok craft. He was the first human to take a protective suit right out into space, making one orbit at an average height of about 241 kilometres (150 miles).

On May 4, of the same year, two American naval officers took a less spectacular but equally hazardous trip to test space suits under hair-raisingly real conditions.

Commander Malcolm Ross and Lieutenant Commander Victor Prather, Jnr. rode to a height of 34.6 kilometres (21.5 miles) over the Gulf of Mexico in a frail aluminium gondola under a giant helium-filled polythene balloon. At their maximum altitude of 34,668 metres (113,740 feet), the two men sat for two hours while the gondola slowly spun around, giving them an unequalled view of the whole Southern United States. The suits did their job but one of the experimenters died, his life taken not by the new enemy space, but by one of the oldest foes of human beings – the sea. At the end of the flight, they were hoisted from the gondola by helicopters. Prather slipped from his hoist and drowned despite the frantic efforts of frogmen to save him.

The next day, Alan Shepard, also a Navy man, took the first American space ride in the tiny Mercury capsule in which he shot into a sub-orbital test ride. The suits for the Mercury programmes were made by the Goodrich Rubber Company who had made Wiley Post's pioneer-

ing gear in 1934–5, using as a basis the same link-net material which had been so successful in the X-15 spaceplane suits.

The Mercury suit had to be proof against the loss of air pressure inside the capsule and had several new tasks to perform. Its helmet protected the ears against the blistering noise of rocket engines and it contained an inner cooling layer to shield against the rise in temperature on re-entry into the atmosphere. For launch and re-entry, the suit was sealed with the helmet visor closed. During flight it was open and the cabin temperature kept to about 21°C (70°F).

The last, long Mercury flight was made by Gordon Cooper on 15–16 May 1963 and on June 16, more history was made by a Russian when the 26 year-old Valentina Tereshkova went into orbit for three days, the first and only woman space pilot, so far.

* * *

Gemini was the code name for the next stepping stone to the moon. Mercury had tested some basic techniques, now the two-man flights would find out if a moonflight was medically and technically feasible. Two of the main experiments would show if men could live and work in pressure suits for days at a time and if accurate, orbital rendezvous was possible with two spacecraft.

On 18 March 1965, five days before the first Gemini launch, Russia put a two-man craft into space – Voskhod 2, flown by Alexei Leonov (above) and Pavel Belyayer. The craft was fitted with an airlock tunnel leading to a hatch which opened on to space itself and Leonov's suit equipped him for the first walk in space.

For ten minutes he floated above the earth while the spacecraft rolled and twisted gently to the tugging of his umbilical lifelines. It was Gemini 4 which took Jim McDivitt and Ed White into orbit for America's first space-walk. The Gemini suit was developed as the programme progressed to allow greater comfort for the crews on long flights. (On Gemini 7, Borman and Lovell wore lightweight suits with big, soft hoods replacing the conventional tight helmets.) These new outfits protected the astronauts from decompression, heat, cold, radiation and the one-in-a-million chance of being struck by a bullet-like micrometeorite.

From inside, it consisted of ventilated underwear, a 'comfort layer', the pressure bladder, the link-net restraint layer and three outer strengthening layers with an aluminium heat-insulating layer sandwiched between – very necessary to shield the wearer against 95°C (203°F) on his sunlight side and minus 57°C (−135°F) on the shadow side.

Like Leonov, White was elated by floating above such an expanse and it took much effort from anxious controllers and his Commander, McDivitt, to talk White into returning to the capsule.

The suit had worked and more extended 'walks' could now be made to see how a man would take increasing exposure to weightless working and how hard and accurately he could work in a suit. The star performer in this exercise was Astronaut Edwin E. Aldrin, Jnr. He successfully performed three EVA (extra-vehicular activity, in the jargon of space-flight) operations totalling 5.5 hours on Gemini 12, the

last mission in the series. While doctors on the ground watched his body's every reaction, he carried out a series of complicated and delicate tasks around the spacecraft and its docked Agena target vehicle with no noticeable fatigue and without overtaxing the suit's support systems.

On this flight, three lessons were learnt. The value of handholds and points at which the astronaut could anchor himself while working, the value of long rest periods and the importance of the underwater 'weightless' training and rehearsals on earth.

The way ahead to a moon landing was opening. What was once merely a dream was becoming a possibility.

In 1935 when Wiley Post was making his pioneering stratospheric flights, two very young Americans, five year-old Edwin E. Aldrin Jnr. and four year-old Neil A. Armstrong, were just beginning to take a juvenile interest in flying.

Thirty-four years later, when they set a weird flying machine down on the moon, they were wearing suits which were the result of much dedicated research and a lot of money. The bulky 'snowman' outfits in which they jogged and bounced across the grey dust were reputed to cost two million dollars. They were cheap at the price, being complete self-contained life support systems, little 'homes-from-home' on an alien world.

Even the clearest pictures of the Apollo exploration give no hint of the deadly place the moon is for mankind. The temperature, because of the lack of any atmosphere to give an insulating 'greenhouse effect' varies between $+100°C$ ($217°F$) and $-150°C$ ($-302°F$) even in the early lunar morning The same lack of atmosphere allows the full blast of the sun's radiation and a rain of micrometeorites to strike straight at the surface.

So a man must be protected from all these dangers and against the heat generated by his body, plus the necessity to have the carbon dioxide and moisture removed from the canned oxygen he breathes and rebreathes. These requirements had to be met with a design which would still allow the wearer to walk, climb and handle tools and equipment while the suit was pressurised. Over the years many improvements and refinements have been made to meet the requirements of the astronaut.

* * *

The Apollo suit was subjected to much development during its career on the moon and the Apollo 2 gear was different from that used later in the series, culminating in the long excursions of Schmitt and Cernan on the Apollo 17 mission. The most obvious improvement was in the length of time the suit could support its wearer on the moon's surface.

Three basic units made up the suit. From inside, these were (a) a liquid cooling garment which used circulated water in the maze of tiny pipes to carry away the body's heat, (b) the pressure suit itself completely enclosing the wearer with the addition of a 'goldfish bowl' clear helmet and (c) pressure gloves with soft silicon rubber tips to allow some sort of artificial 'fingertip feel'. This suit contained a complete head-to-toe ventilation system.

The third, outer garment giving the familiar 'snowman with a glass face' appearance, was the many-layered overall designed to protect against extreme temperatures, strikes by micrometeorites and any damage to the all-important pressure suit. Lunar overshoes were worn on top of all this gear to separate the feet thoroughly from the surface. They consisted of 25 layers of aluminium film and cloth sewn to a thick silicon rubber sole.

In all, three helmets were used. A light soft leather cap worn from start to finish carrying earphones and mini-microphones, the pressure helmet and, for moonwalking, a bulbous outer helmet with two visors, one to protect the pressure helmet, a second gold-filmed to guard against solar radiation.

On his back, the explorer wore a glass fibre container which supplied oxygen for breathing, suit pressurisation and ventilation, oxygen and water for body-cooling and a separate unit to scrub the breathing oxygen clean for it to be re-used.

This 'space tortoise' with his home on his back could still walk about, fiddle with delicate instruments, drive Moon Rovers and kick rocks down hills – all thanks to the ingenious design of the suit, the long and arduous training beforehand and the low gravity conditions on the Moon.

The first man to trust the whole assembly with his life in deep space was an astronaut on his first mission. This was Russell 'Rusty' Schweichart of Apollo 9, the earth orbital flight which made the first tests of many lunar landing devices including the lander itself and the docking procedure. Schweichart, unlike the earlier Gemini and Voskhod space-walkers, had no umbilical lines when he climbed out of the lunar module hatch and stood on the tiny platform outside.

Today, Skylab astronauts use similar units with umbilical lines to clamber about the outside of their vehicle for routine maintenance tasks and photography. On Christmas Day, 1973, the third Skylab crew set a new spacewalk endurance record by operating outside for seven hours.

Skylab is also testing the first unit designed to allow a suited man to travel and manoeuvre himself in space with precision instead of merely floating from one handhold to the next. This means that the astronaut is able to carry out minor repairs to the exterior of his ship.

Meanwhile full-pressure suits are still in use every day for flights in the atmosphere, notably by such aircraft as the Lockheed SR. 71 'Spy-Plane'.

These sinister-looking aircraft are among the 'hottest' ships in the sky today, and capable of cruising at well over 3,218 kilometres (2,000 miles) per hour at heights of up to 30,480 metres (100,000 feet) for long periods. Preparations for a flight start the day before and the briefing procedure includes a full medical examination and pressure suit check. The pilots who fly these planes must be 100 per cent fit and alert.

Continued from page 45

Space Cadet

In the year 2805 AD, manned space-craft were able to soar at fantastic and almost unbelievable speeds to the far corners of the galaxy. Thanks to her glorious Royal Space Force, Britain was queen of space, just as she had once been queen of the seas – but from the trackless voids of the skies, unknown dangers were always threatening the peace of the planet Earth.

One such danger threatened now. Just before dawn one day, a strange craft landed in a remote and unpopulated part of the Scottish highlands. The intruder came from the far-off and warlike planet of Tarsen, and it brought . . . trouble!

When the craft zoomed skywards again, it left behind three sturdy lads clad in the normal dress of the 29th century. These boys had come from Tarsen on a desperate mission.

Next day, the three youths from Tarsen made their way into the city of Glasgow. There, they called at the recruiting office of the Royal Space Force.

recruiting cent

Join the RSF as a Cadet great opportunities for youths from 11 - 16 years.

Presenting cunningly-forged identity papers, the boys from Tarsen volunteered for service in the RSF. In due course, they were allowed to sit for the stiff examination for entry into the Royal Space Force Academy at Portsmouth.

They found it simple to pass the exam. Their sophisticated brains found the questions easy.

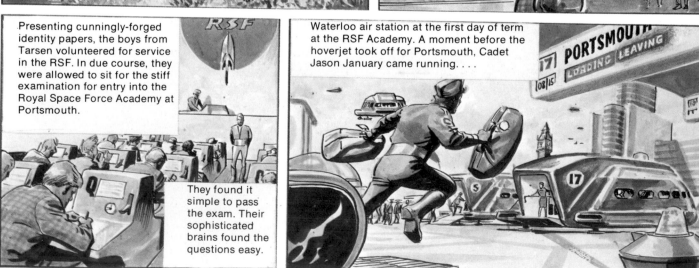

Waterloo air station at the first day of term at the RSF Academy. A moment before the hoverjet took off for Portsmouth, Cadet Jason January came running. . . .

PORTSMOUTH
LOADING LEAVING

. . . just in time, Jason threw his bags aboard the bus and leapt inside . . . to find that the bags had knocked over his best chum and classmate, genial Nick Ringold.

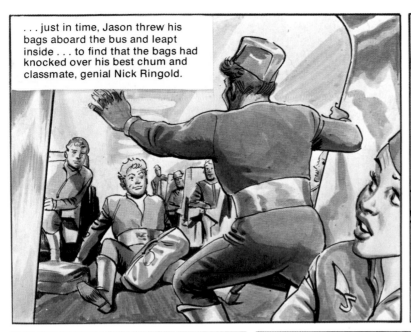

Cheery Nick Ringold took the accident in good part and introduced Jason to a brand-new cadet whom he had just met. 'It's an honour to meet you, Jason,' said the newcomer. 'Nick has been telling me all about you. My name is James Starr.'

As he shook hands with the new cadet, Jason thought what a likeable lad he seemed. Little did he suspect that James Starr was an intruder from the enemy planet of Tarsen.

There was another cadet on the flight. Tom Bolt, the bully of the 'Ranger' class was the sworn enemy of Jason and Nick. 'I'll give January a sticky greeting,' sniggered Bolt to himself. As he spoke, he produced a large tin of treacle from the bag he had brought with him.

A few moments later, Bolt's grinning face appeared over the back of the seat. The treacle began to ooze forth out of the upturned tin. . . .

The cadets were unaware of Bolt. But the Tarsens had a superhuman sense of danger. James Starr knew what was happening!

James Starr re-acted absolutely instinctively. Without pausing to consider the situation even for the briefest moment, he hurled his heavy book over his head.

Tom Bolt slumped down into his seat, writhing with discomfort as the sticky mess trickled down his face and the back of his neck. 'Well done, James,' laughed Jason. 'You think swiftly!'

And so, by the time they alighted near the Royal Space Force Academy, the boy from outer space who had come to Earth to work under-cover for its ultimate destruction was already a friend of two of the famous academy's brightest cadets.

'These two earthlings are a pair of utter simpletons,' thought James Starr. 'I will, no doubt, find them useful to me in the days to come.'

Unaware that a terrible menace was in their midst, Jason January and his classmates began the winter term in their usual high spirits. 'Here he comes!' rang out the cry on the first morning, and a score of mischievous and boisterous cadets raced to occupy their seats.

A row of solemn faces greeted their instructor when he entered. This was Wing-Commander Paddy Keane, the hero of the first manned-flight to Venus and the idol of his class. 'Morning, lads!' growled the peppery Wingco. 'Morning, sir!' replied the Rangers.

Unsuspectingly, Keane lifted the lid of his desk . . . and from the transistor tape recorder which had been concealed within came the voices of the Ranger class singing.

Wingco Keane's single eye swept the grins from the faces of the class. 'Very amusing,' he said, with a glance in Jason January's direction. 'I can very easily guess just who was the instigator of this beginning-of-term greeting!'

The Rangers knew from grim experience just how far they could go with their genial . . . but tough . . . instructor. That was the first prank of the term . . . and the last!

Next, Wingco Keane introduced three new members of the class. 'Reading from left to right, these are James Starr, Henry Bream and Sam Craddock,' he said, in his usual terse manner. 'I know that you'll make them all very welcome!'

Jason, of course, had already met James Starr on the hoverjet ride from Waterloo to Portsmouth. The two boys exchanged a friendly grin and a wink.

The first lesson that morning was an introductory course of instruction on one of the Royal Space Force Academy's very latest space craft. The class watched with absorbed interest and close attention as Wing-Commander Keane pointed out in great detail the top security information and data regarding the most modern and secret weapon.

None followed the lesson more closely than the new cadets – for a good reason.

Like James Starr, Henry Bream and Sam Craddock were also spies from the hostile planet of Tarsen. At the end of the morning classes, Jason January took the three of them to the Royal Space Force Academy's vast hangar in order to show them the training craft.

Afterwards, James Starr walked swiftly away on his own to a quiet and isolated part of the academy grounds. Arriving there, he halted beside a tree and, looking carefully around him, surveyed the whole area to make sure that he had not been followed.

Assured that he was unobserved, the new cadet took a small packet from his pocket and assembled it into a short-wave transmitter of fabulous power. He spoke quietly. 'Calling Tarsen,' he said. 'This is agent Z reporting on our earth mission. . . .'

But Starr had been followed, after all. Tom Bolt, the bully of the Ranger class, had carefully trailed the new cadet, hoping to catch him when he was on his own.

'I'll give that cheeky new kid a thrashing for siding with January,' hissed Bolt. 'But whatever does he think he's doing, crouching there?'

Tom Bolt, in his turn, had been followed! The second spy from Tarsen who called himself Henry Bream was only a few paces distant. Watching from behind the trunk of a full-grown tree, he sized up the situation, and then, with calm deliberation, produced a strangely-shaped object from his pocket and aimed it at the unsuspecting Bolt.

Tom Bolt crawled cautiously forward. The bully of the 'Ranger' class was intent upon finding out exactly what James Starr was doing. Meanwhile, Henry Bream threw a strange dart at Bolt's back.

The cowardly Bolt, who had set out to beat up somebody he took to be an innocent new recruit, had unwittingly pitted himself against adversaries far more menacing and dangerous than anything he had ever envisaged. For the time being, however, he was to realize none of this. When the strange dart struck him on the shoulder, he felt nothing at all. Nor did he see or sense the cloud of dark red vapour which the disintegrating dart released.

The bully of the 'Ranger' class breathed the vapour and, without so much as a moan, fell forward upon his face. A few moments later, the dart-thrower stepped out from behind the tree to join his companion from Tarsen.

'Did he see me using the radio?' asked the one who called himself James Starr. 'If he did, he will remember nothing of it,' replied the other. 'When he recovers consciousness, his mind will be completely confused.'

Leaving Tom Bolt where he lay, the two young spies walked back to the academy. Starr had received news from Tarsen. 'They give us no more than six weeks to learn Earth's space secrets,' he said. 'There's not a moment to lose!'

At dinner time in the great hall of the academy that evening, Jason January took his usual place at the dining-table next to his closest chum Nick Ringold. And then it happened! 'Great Scott! Just look at Bolt!' exclaimed Nick. 'What does he think he's doing?'

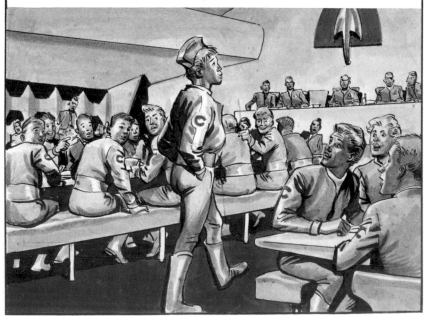

It was unheard of for a cadet to stroll into the hall with his hands in his pockets. But worse was to follow. Before the horrified eyes of everyone present, Bolt sat down and put his feet up on the table which was reserved for officers!

Portly Commodore Prendergast, the head of the Royal Space Force Academy, could only sit and watch in dumb-struck astonishment as the cadet sitting at his side reached out for the gravy boat. Then, putting the vessel to his lips, Tom Bolt took a hearty swallow.

The infuriated Commodore Prendergast found his voice at last. 'Have you taken leave of your senses, boy?' he bawled. 'Leave this table at once and report to the guard-room!'

With slow and insolent deliberation, the bully of the 'Ranger' class lowered the gravy boat from his mouth. 'I don't know who you are, fatty, but I don't like your face,' he snapped. 'You're ugly, did you know that?'

With these words, Tom Bolt poured what was left of the gravy over Commodore Prendergast.

Only three people in the hall knew that Tom Bolt's amazing behaviour was caused by the strange red vapour he had inhaled. These three were, of course, the cadets who were really spies from Tarsen.

Leaping to his feet, Commodore Prendergast wiped the sticky gravy from his face and pointed a shaking finger at Bolt, who appeared to be completely unconcerned.

'Never in all my years of service have I seen or heard of such insolent and outrageous behaviour to a senior officer!' he thundered. 'Take that cadet to the guard room. His punishment will be severe!'

Still under the influence of the vapour he had inhaled, Tom Bolt had no idea what was happening. 'Take your hands off me!' he yelled. 'How dare you throw me out before I've had my dinner. Where's the manager?'

The three boys from Tarsen held a whispered conference together. 'The effect of the vapour will wear off soon,' said one. 'That fool will have forgotten everything. He will give us no more trouble.'

'I shall never come into your rotten restaurant again!' shouted Tom Bolt, as he was led away by two armed cadets.

At the end of the day's classes, Jason showed the new cadets around. 'This is our standard training craft,' he said. 'I'll take you for a couple of earth orbits in her tomorrow if you like.' The three spies accepted the invitation.

Starr's interest was aroused by a locked and guarded hangar. 'That houses the new experimental space-fighter,' said Jason. 'It's out of bounds, I'm afraid.'

An hour after lights out had sounded in the Rangers' dormitory, James Starr slid silently and stealthily out of his bed. His two companions also rose, and all three of them crept with great care between the rows of sleeping cadets.

From their lockers, the three spies took out short jackets made of some strange, glittering and silver material. Donning his jacket, Starr climbed on to the locker room window-sill and stood poised to jump.

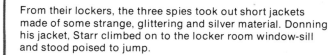

He leapt . . . and the others followed him. And the three boys from Tarsen drifted silently through the night air above the sleeping academy. The material of their jackets was impregnated with a wonderful material found only on their home planet . . . and it defied the laws of gravity!

They alighted on the dome of the forbidden hangar, and prised open the fanlight. Nobody was about to catch a glimpse of the three youthful spies as they made their entry into the building which contained such a vital secret.

Moving downwards with the effortless ease of swimmers gliding about in clear waters, the three spies finally alighted on the floor of the hangar. Their eyes glittered with interest as they stood and surveyed the sleek secret fighter which shone in the bright moonlight streaming in from the fanlight above.

'Get to work. There is no time to waste,' gritted Starr. 'Before we leave here, we have to examine this craft, memorize every single detail of its design and construction, and radio all the information we have been able to gather to our masters back on Tarsen. Every second is vital lest we should be disturbed.'

Outside, the portly figure of Commodore Prendergast, the head of the Royal Space Force Academy, appeared out of the gloom. The guards on duty at the doors of the forbidden hangar sprang to attention and saluted their commander smartly.

Commodore Prendergast was well-known for his habit of prowling around the grounds of the Academy during the night to see that everything was in order.

The sound of a door opening caused the three spies from Tarsen to turn in alarm from their examination of the secret space fighter. 'Somebody's coming in,' hissed Starr, in tones of sibilant menace. 'Whoever he is, he must be dealt with. Nobody must be allowed to jeopardize the success of our mission.'

Commodore Prendergast entered and closed the door behind him. 'What the blazes are you doing?' he gasped when he saw the boys.

James Starr's re-actions were lightning fast. In a flash, he jerked a small object from his pocket and sent the jet-propelled dart hissing through the air towards Commodore Prendergast.

The Commodore fell when the dart struck him and disintegrated into a red vapour. 'Good! He is now unconscious,' grunted Starr. 'He will remember nothing.'

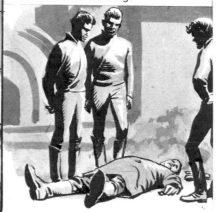

'Let's get out of here,' said the spies' leader. Aided by their gravity-defying jackets, they floated to the top of the high dome, where the skylight stood open.

Minutes later, the three spies from the planet of Tarsen were gliding back into the window of the 'Ranger' class locker room which they had left open earlier.

It was past three a.m. when the Commodore emerged from the secret hangar. 'Good-morning, sir,' said the guards. But Commodore Prendergast said not a word. He walked off with his eyes fixed dully ahead of him.

After breakfast, the cadets were summoned to the great hall. They gathered in a buzz of excitement. All knew what was coming. Tom Bolt was to be tried and punished by Commodore Prendergast for his fantastic behaviour at dinner the day before.

Unknown to anyone but the three spies, Bolt had also fallen a victim to the red vapour which robbed a person of his memory. Now the bully had a vague recollection of what had happened and his heart quaked.

'Did I really tell the Head that I didn't like his face . . . and then pour gravy all over him?' he faltered. Jason January grinned. 'You certainly did,' he replied.

Then Commodore Prendergast appeared, and Tom Bolt was brought up before him. But it was obvious that the Head of the Space Academy was not his usual self.

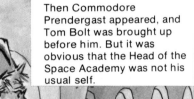

Looking about him with an angry expression, Commodore Prendergast said: 'Why have I been fetched from my bed to come here? What a disgusting way to treat a guest at this hotel!'

With these words, the Commodore turned on his heel and walked out of the great hall.

'What are you staring at?' he demanded. 'Have you never seen a dressing-gown before?'

After the amazing behaviour of the Head, life at the Academy was slow to settle down to its usual routine. It was midday before Jason reminded the boys from Tarsen of his promise. 'Do you still want to come for a few orbits in the training craft?' he asked.

The three spies readily agreed. As the four walked towards the space craft, Starr took one of the memory-destroying darts from his pocket. 'We will use this on January during the flight,' he hissed to his companions. 'For a very special reason!'

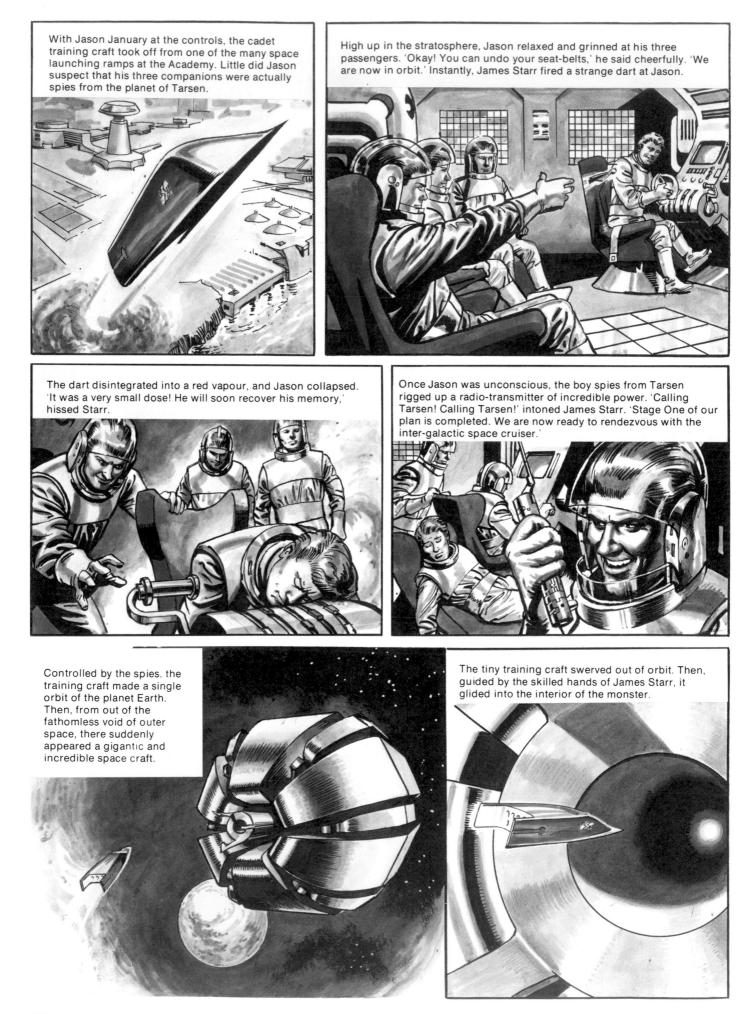

With Jason January at the controls, the cadet training craft took off from one of the many space launching ramps at the Academy. Little did Jason suspect that his three companions were actually spies from the planet of Tarsen.

High up in the stratosphere, Jason relaxed and grinned at his three passengers. 'Okay! You can undo your seat-belts,' he said cheerfully. 'We are now in orbit.' Instantly, James Starr fired a strange dart at Jason.

The dart disintegrated into a red vapour, and Jason collapsed. 'It was a very small dose! He will soon recover his memory,' hissed Starr.

Once Jason was unconscious, the boy spies from Tarsen rigged up a radio-transmitter of incredible power. 'Calling Tarsen! Calling Tarsen!' intoned James Starr. 'Stage One of our plan is completed. We are now ready to rendezvous with the inter-galactic space cruiser.'

Controlled by the spies, the training craft made a single orbit of the planet Earth. Then, from out of the fathomless void of outer space, there suddenly appeared a gigantic and incredible space craft.

The tiny training craft swerved out of orbit. Then, guided by the skilled hands of James Starr, it glided into the interior of the monster.

Later, in a vast compartment as big and impressive as the vaults of a cathedral, the three spies from Tarsen stood and bowed respectfully before the commanding figure of the war-lord of their planet. 'So far, you have done well. Make your report!' he grated in a harsh metallic voice.

Briefly, Starr told of his discoveries on Earth. 'The new space fighter is the key. Bring it to me intact!' said his leader.

The three young spies returned to the Royal Space Force craft, and, on the way back to Earth, Jason January recovered consciousness. 'That trip seems to have passed very swiftly,' he said drowsily.

No sooner had they landed than a glittering and impressive cavalcade of hover-cars glided silently into the grounds of the Academy. 'Hello! What's going on?' grunted Jason.

The powerful figure in the leading car stood up. 'It's the Marshal of the Space Force,' gasped Jason.

Bugles shrilled from end to end of the academy grounds, and the duty officer had the presence of mind to call out the ceremonial guard of honour. 'Where is your commanding officer?' barked the Marshal.

Commodore Prendergast appeared. The head of the academy glared at the Marshal. 'They dragged me out of my bath to see you!' he roared. 'Who are you?'

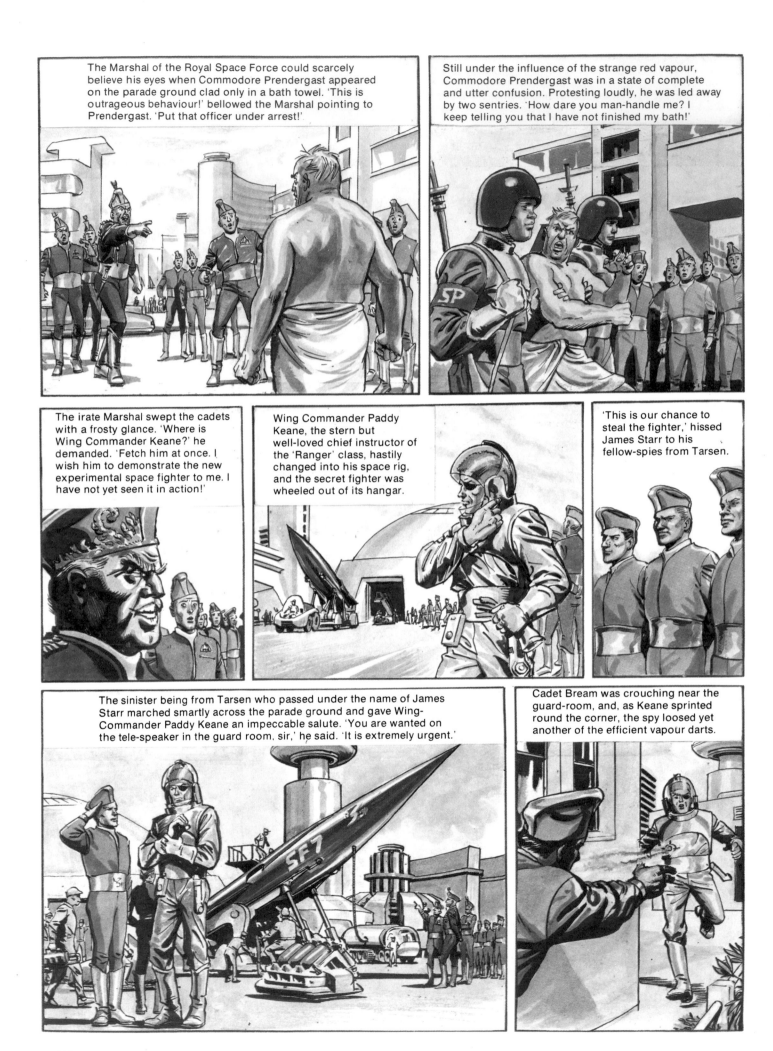

The Marshal of the Royal Space Force could scarcely believe his eyes when Commodore Prendergast appeared on the parade ground clad only in a bath towel. 'This is outrageous behaviour!' bellowed the Marshal pointing to Prendergast. 'Put that officer under arrest!'

Still under the influence of the strange red vapour, Commodore Prendergast was in a state of complete and utter confusion. Protesting loudly, he was led away by two sentries. 'How dare you man-handle me? I keep telling you that I have not finished my bath!'

The irate Marshal swept the cadets with a frosty glance. 'Where is Wing Commander Keane?' he demanded. 'Fetch him at once. I wish him to demonstrate the new experimental space fighter to me. I have not yet seen it in action!'

Wing Commander Paddy Keane, the stern but well-loved chief instructor of the 'Ranger' class, hastily changed into his space rig, and the secret fighter was wheeled out of its hangar.

'This is our chance to steal the fighter,' hissed James Starr to his fellow-spies from Tarsen.

The sinister being from Tarsen who passed under the name of James Starr marched smartly across the parade ground and gave Wing-Commander Paddy Keane an impeccable salute. 'You are wanted on the tele-speaker in the guard room, sir,' he said. 'It is extremely urgent.'

Cadet Bream was crouching near the guard-room, and, as Keane sprinted round the corner, the spy loosed yet another of the efficient vapour darts.

One breath of the red vapour in the dart and Keane fell unconscious. 'Get into his suit, Bream!' said Starr. 'You're taking the secret fighter to Tarsen!'

A few minutes later, a space-suited figure was seen walking swiftly towards the sleek fighter. 'About time, too!' snapped the Marshal. 'How much longer am I to be kept waiting?'

Bream slid into the narrow cockpit and glanced at the controls. He had only seen the fighter once before, but his super-human mind had memorized every detail of the mechanism.

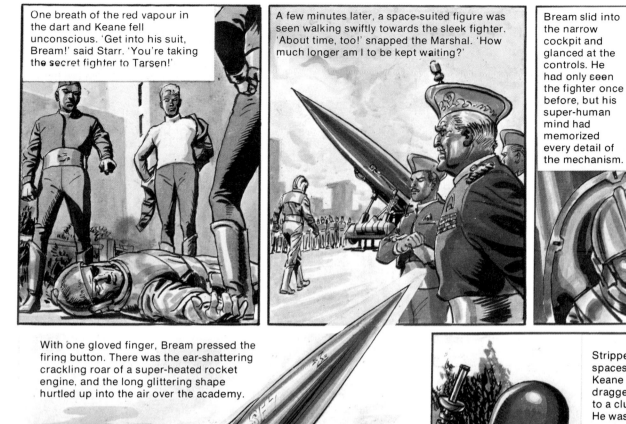

With one gloved finger, Bream pressed the firing button. There was the ear-shattering crackling roar of a super-heated rocket engine, and the long glittering shape hurtled up into the air over the academy.

Stripped of his spacesuit, Paddy Keane had been dragged by the spies to a clump of bushes. He was discovered by a patrolling guard . . . who immediately rushed to raise the alarm.

The news spread through the academy like wildfire: 'Paddy Keane is not piloting that fighter. Somebody has stolen the greatest secret the Royal Space Force has ever possessed!'

Cadet Jason January raced for the Rangers' space craft. 'There's not much hope of catching that fighter in this old crock,' he thought. 'But it's our only chance!'

The gigantic and elaborate control room at the Royal Space Force Academy buzzed with frantic activity. Directed by the Senior Controller of the establishment, the operators on duty were swift to focus their tele-radar equipment. They soon located the two fast-disappearing space craft.

The Marshal of the Royal Space Force snorted with contempt. 'How can that young cadet catch up with the fastest fighter on earth?' he growled. 'January has a slim chance,' replied the controller. 'The fighter might run out of fuel. It is only carrying enough for half-an-hour of space flight!'

High in the stratosphere above the Southern Atlantic, Jason January was crouched over the controls of his craft, watching the glow of the fighter's rockets far ahead. 'I'm losing him,' groaned Jason.

In the stolen secret plane, the spy who called himself Henry Bream was speaking urgently into the long-range radio with which the craft was equipped.

'Calling Tarsen!' he said. 'I have the secret fighter. I am ready to rendezvous with our inter-galactic cruiser over the south pole of the Earth.'

Seconds later, exactly half an hour after take-off, the engines of the fighter faded, and the spy felt the controls go dead.

Jason stared in alarm to see the fighter diving out of control towards the white continent of Antarctica. 'If that chap doesn't use his ejector gear, he'll be killed,' he cried.

It was soon all over. With the speed of a descending meteor, the experimental fighter crashed down through the pack ice.

Jason landed his craft and damaged it beyond all repair. Then, after donning a cold-resisting suit, he scrambled across the ice-cap until he reached the experimental fighter.

Peering into the cockpit, Jason saw the pilot lying unconscious. To his surprise, he found himself gazing at his class mate. 'Great Scott! It's Henry Bream!' he exclaimed. 'Why on earth should he want to steal the ultra-secret new fighter?'

And then, for some strange reason, a sixth sense impelled him to look up into the sky above his head.

Slowly it descended out of the heavens towards Jason January . . . a menacing shape that seemed to shut out the slanting rays of the Antarctic sun.

Before Jason's unbelieving eyes, the monster craft alighted upon a tall icy peak. As it did so, an intense and vivid ray shone down from the underparts of the great space ship. And the heat generated by the orange ray melted the peak of ice beneath it!

Stung into action by a chill and numbing dread, Jason January dragged the unconscious Henry Bream from the cockpit of the space craft, and struggled with him towards a nearby crevasse.

From his place of concealment the young cadet watched as a large party of armed men emerged from the monster craft, and marched like a column of ants towards the crashed training craft.

The warriors of Tarsen tramped like so many mindless automatons across the rutted surface of the ice-cap and halted when they reached the ruined remains of the training craft in which Jason January had crashed. Then, they broke ranks and clustered around the 'Ranger' craft, while their officers considered the situation.

From his hiding-place in the ice, Jason gazed upon the scene. 'Who are these men?' he mused to himself. 'Where in the galaxy do they come from? How did they know that my craft was here? And what's their interest in it?' He could think of no answers to his questions.

At a sharp order from one of the Tarsen officers, the jib of a gigantic crane emerged on caterpillar tracks from the interior of the massive ship. Jason's tiny training craft was drawn up into the air by magnetic force.

Completely dwarfed by the colossal bulk of the space ship from Tarsen, the little training craft pivoted on the end of the crane and was deposited in one of the space monster's mighty holds. Then the crane trundled back into the ship.

Jason January watched in awe as the powerful throbbing of mighty engines lifted the huge and unearthly shape up from the ice-cap into the clear blue Antarctic sky.

Soon the giant craft was out of sight. It was then that Jason came out of his hiding-place and saw that he was marooned.

Then the space cadet was jolted off his feet as . . . with an ear-splitting crack . . . a great gap appeared in the surface. 'Good grief!' muttered Jason. 'It's a thaw! The ice-cap is breaking up! The experimental fighter is lost.'

Within a few hours, Jason January and the spy from Tarsen were isolated on a small ice-floe which was soon caught up in a powerful and relentless Antarctic current and whirled helplessly into the green uncharted waters of the remote and terrible region.

'Where are we?' faltered Henry Bream, recovering consciousness, and gazing up to see Jason. Jason stared at him grimly. 'We're in big trouble,' he replied. 'Just who are you? Why did you steal the fighter?'

Jason's question was greeted by a sullen silence. From his pocket emergency kit, Jason produced a fishing-line. 'There will be fish for supper,' he said. 'But, if you don't talk, you don't eat.'

Presently, with the aid of a miniature stove, Jason was grilling a fine fish. 'Changed your mind yet?' he grinned. Bream licked his lips hungrily. 'Yes,' he said grudgingly. 'I'll talk . . .'

Meanwhile far up in the stratosphere, aboard the giant Tarsen space ship, the fearsome war-lord of that forbidding planet was engaged in a close study of the captured training cadet craft . . . thinking that it was a specimen of Earth's latest secret fighter.

At length, the war-lord snorted with contempt. 'If this is the best that Earth can produce, our task will be easy,' he said. 'Send a message to Tarsen at once. Tell them to let the invasion of Earth begin!'

Within minutes, super long-wave radio beams were flashing the awesome message to the far-off warlike planet. On the surface of Tarsen, crews of warriors raced to climb aboard the assembled rows of gigantic fighting ships. They needed no time to plan or organize. What was about to happen had long been contemplated. All Tarsen had been awaiting was the word.

The roar of mighty engines shattered the silence. The invasion was under way!

The spy who called himself Henry Bream told how Tarsen was planning to invade the earth. 'What does it matter if you know?' he said. 'Neither of us is going to get out of this alive.' Jason's jaw set firmly. 'That's what you think, my friend,' he answered, with grim determination.

While the two boys crouched on the ice floe, several hours passed slowly. Then suddenly, a monstrous shape arose from the deep. 'Look out!' shouted Jason to his companion. 'It's a killer whale!'

The ferocious killer whale did not even see the two boys, but one accidental flick of its great tail shattered the ice floe to fragments. Jason and Bream were flung into the freezing sea.

Bream had been struck on the head by a heavy block of ice. Senseless, he sank deep beneath the surface, but Jason January dived down after him and managed to grasp him by the ankle.

Jason fought his way to the surface and held the Tarsen spy's head clear of the water. 'In this low temperature, our insulated suits should keep us alive for an hour or so,' thought Jason. 'After that, we'll be done for.'

The hour was nearly up when Jason saw condensation trails in the sky. 'Rescue craft . . . looking for us,' he cried. 'I must release the yellow dye from its pouch in my suit. It will help them spot us.'

Minutes later, from the control cabin of one of the rescue craft of the Royal Space Academy, Jason's closest friend, Nick Ringold, saw the great patch of yellow dye spreading slowly over the waters of the icy sea. 'Look! There they are!' he cried.

84

The craft landed on the sea and the two boys were helped aboard. 'Thank heavens we found you, Jason,' murmured Nick. 'But why did Bream steal the secret fighter?' Jason brushed the question aside. 'Take me back to the Academy,' he cried. 'It means life or death for the whole world!'

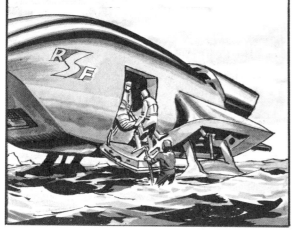

That night, Jason kept watch over the unconscious Bream in a Portsmouth hospital. Sharing his vigil were a number of senior officers of the Royal Space Force, including no less a personage than the Marshal himself.

The long hours dragged slowly by, and then Bream opened his eyes.

Bream fixed his gaze on Jason January. 'You saved my life,' he said weakly, 'and, in return, I am going to save yours. Now listen carefully to me . . .'

Twenty-four hours later, the mighty invasion fleet from the warlike planet of Tarsen swept down towards the earth. There were hordes of the mighty craft and they were travelling at a velocity close to the speed of light.

Suddenly, without the slightest warning, the entire fleet stopped dead in space as if gripped by a gigantic invisible hand.

Panic reigned aboard the leading craft. 'The people on Earth are jamming the radio beam along which we are travelling,' hissed the leader. 'We shall have to return to Tarsen.'

In the central astro-radio station, Jason January stood and watched the great fleet disappearing from the tele-radar screens. 'So our transmissions destroyed their beam,' he murmured 'Bream told us what to do.'

So ended the threat to earth, and the astonishing events that had taken place at the Royal Space Academy were explained. The repentant boy-spies from Tarsen were pardoned by the Director of Space Force I, and Jason was decorated with the Space Force Gallantry Cross.

Continued on page 99

Continued on page 99

Crisis in Space

For hundreds of years, gallant explorers have roamed the Earth's surface, willing to gamble their very lives to discover what lay beyond the distant blue mountains, what unknown territories existed beyond the horizons of the oceans.

Gambled their lives – yes, and lost them.

Space has sadly claimed its victims, too, but upon a certain April day in 1970, death was robbed of its intended victims.

Keen brains, great technical skill and excellent physical condition are not all the attributes demanded of an astronaut. He must also possess an ability to keep an ice-cold control of his reflexes even when faced by that most awesome peril – an emergency in space.

Way back in April 1970, the Space Mission Control scientists in Houston, Texas, were readying-up the Americans' third landing on the Moon.

Astronauts Lovell, Haise and Swigert had been selected for the mission. Confidently they boarded the Apollo 13 spacecraft.

All seemed to be going well as messages crackled back and forth between the technicians in Mission Control and the astronauts speeding towards the Moon when suddenly the confident hopes of the land-based scientists were shattered by a quiet but urgent:

'Hey! We've got a problem here!'

Everybody's heart missed a beat. A problem? What sort of problem?

'Hey! We've got a problem here!' The voice was so calm but Apollo 13 was now 18,668 kilometres (11,600 miles) from Earth. Behind that emotionless voice was the fact that an explosion had blown a panel from the service module and cut the astronauts' supplies of oxygen and water.

A moon landing was now impossible although the craft was already being pulled by the Moon's gravity.

Without using the main propulsion system again, the astronauts steered with the engine designed for the moon landing vehicle.

Swiftly the orders went from Houston. The men were told to save light and heat. Next the damaged service module and the life-saving lunar module had to be disposed of, to allow the command module to re-enter the atmosphere unencumbered.

Lovell started the landing craft engine so that the lunar module and command module pushed in the direction of the service module. Simultaneously, Haise fired the explosive bolts that detached the module. Then Lovell reversed the thrust and so pulled away from the service module.

The men entered the command module, warmed up its thrusters and recharged its batteries from power from the lunar module. The connecting tunnel was closed, bolts untied and air pressure in the tunnel pushed the lunar module away.

The six-ton command module fell to Earth at more than 24,944 kilometres (15,500 miles) per hour. Finally, unharmed, the astronauts were floating on the water after their epic journey of 61,958 kilometres (38,500 miles) and the short ill-fated mission of Apollo 13 was over.

Time Travellers

Time-travelling is the simplest occupation in the world. You need no super-scientific devices to do it. Go outside on a clear night and look up at the sky. When you do so, you are travelling through time into the past.

You see the stars, not as they are now, but as they were many years ago. Many of them, in fact, are seen as they were long before Man appeared upon Earth. This is because light, which seems to fill the largest room instantly at the flick of a switch, has a speed limit. That limit is 300,000 kilometres (186,000 miles) per second and nothing is known in the universe which moves faster.

If the sun vanished from the sky, even on the brightest of summer days, our eyes would not warn us of its disappearance until eight minutes afterwards. For this is the length of time light takes to travel the 150 million kilometres (93 million miles) between Earth and Sun. And that distance is trivial compared to the gulf between our solar system and the nearest star, Alpha Centauri. We see this star as it was more than four years ago.

Perhaps, way out in the far depths of space, there may be intelligent beings who can somehow build up a detailed picture from the light-rays reaching them from Earth. If so it might well reveal to them a cloudy jungle-covered globe where giant reptiles still rule.

This sort of knowledge was once of little

interest to anyone other than astronomers and physicists – and possibly science-fiction readers – but the arrival of space flight has changed that situation.

Man did not wait to conquer the Earth, nor even to explore it fully, before reaching out for the Moon. And before his spaceships have landed on Pluto, he may well be aiming a craft at the stars. From this point onward, the ideas that once seemed no more than wild imaginings will be vitally important. For the first inter-stellar ship will fly on a voyage, not only into space, but also into time.

Many designs for an inter-stellar ship have been proposed. Among the more spectacular of these are the 'Noah's Ark' and the ram-jet. Although they represent two very different answers to the problem of covering great distances in time and space, they have one thing in common. Neither can succeed unless some form of space-drive is developed which uses atomic energy, the chemical fuels which have taken astronauts to the Moon being unable to provide sufficient power to carry future adventurers to the stars.

The 'Noah's Ark' design proposes a miniature artificial Earth, intended to carry a crew of several hundred people and to be entirely self-supporting. To overcome such monumental difficulties involved in constructing so huge a vessel, it has been suggested (unbelievable as it may be) that we might use the materials already present in space. An asteroid, one of those irregular masses of rock orbiting between Mars and Jupiter and ranging in size from mere pebbles to bodies 644 kilometres (400 miles) in diameter could be hollowed out and fitted with a suitable propulsion unit. This unit need not be capable of lifting the asteroid-ship into orbit for 'Noah's Ark' would be equipped with smaller craft to ferry her crew to and from the surface of a planet, while she remained permanently in space.

The men and women who set out in such ships will be extraordinarily dedicated people. If the

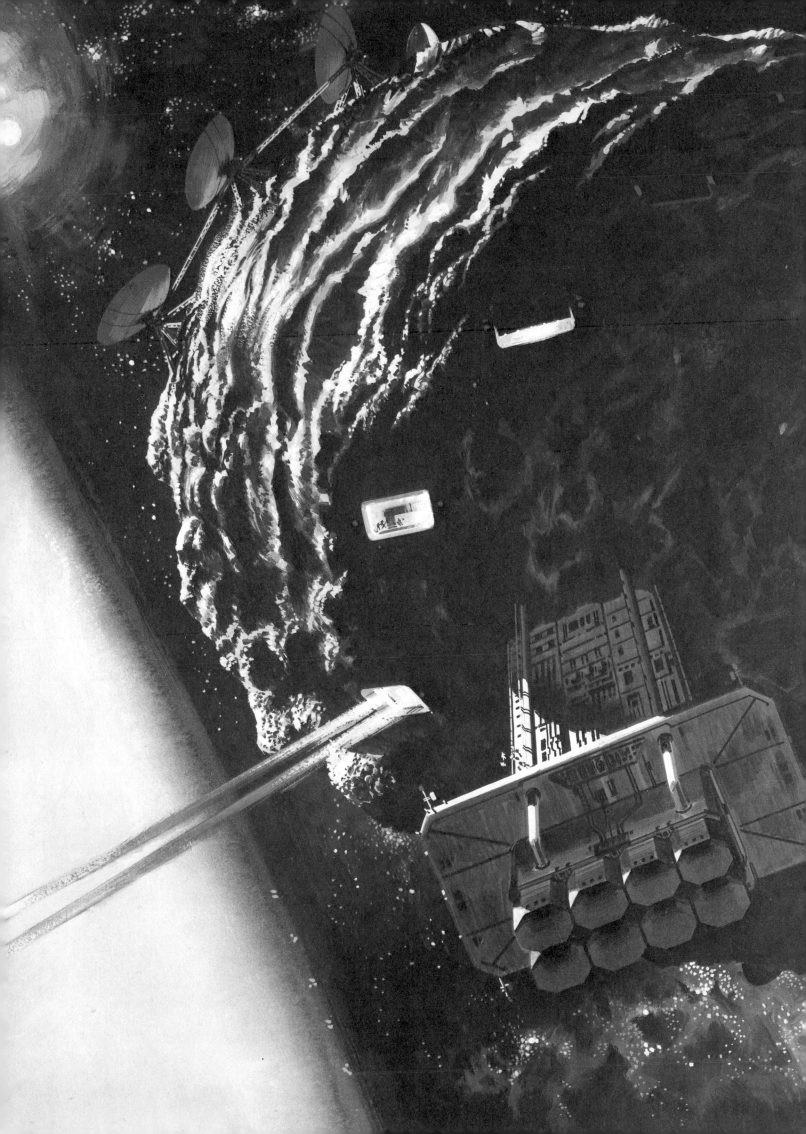

star at which they aim is a very distant one, only their great-great-grandchildren may live to celebrate the Ark's arrival at their destination. It is difficult to imagine that anyone would be willing to undertake such a journey.

Because it offers the possibility of reaching speeds close to that of light, the alternative system – that of the ram-jet – may make it possible for men to reach the stars in their own lifetime. This craft would work by sucking in fuel as it moves forward and expelling it at the rear, in the manner of a jet-plane. But the ram-jet's fuel would not be the jet-plane's air and kerosene. Instead it would feed upon the clouds of hydrogen which fill the spaces between the stars. Although these clouds are so thin that on Earth they would be regarded as an almost perfect vacuum, they would become denser as the speed of the ram-jet increased, just as air 'piles up' before a speeding aircraft to form the well-known 'sound barrier'.

When the atomic motors had set the ship in motion, a colossal scoop, powered by those same motors, would reach out ahead of it to gather in the hydrogen. This scoop would actually be a magnetic field which seized hydrogen atoms and rammed them into the nuclear furnace which would release their tremendous energies. Moving through a universe filled with fuel, the ram-jet would burn it continuously, building up speed in a way denied to any ship which must carry its own supply.

The real trouble for the inter-stellar astronauts will begin when they have learned how to travel almost as fast as light, for peculiar things begin to happen at this point. If for example, a twenty-year old astronaut went into space for a trip at light-speed, leaving his twin brother behind on Earth, he could return after two years to find that his brother was now middle-aged. (See above.) The ship's clocks would have ticked away two years and the crew would be exactly two years older while ten times that number of years had passed on Earth.

When the Americans flew four, highly accurate atomic clocks around the world, they took the average of the time they showed by a clock that stayed on Earth. There were variations but these were so tiny that they were measured in tenths of a second. However, the experiment showed that the clocks that flew eastwards lost time, while those flying westwards gained time.

And so we can travel through time, both to the past and the future, although we have very little choice either way. We see only those portions of the past that are brought to us by the light of the stars.

To see into the future, we must move through space as well as time. Our time machine will be the first inter-stellar ship. The space-time astronauts will always be strangers when they return to Earth from their long voyages, for they will have travelled out of the past. Incredible? Yes. But perhaps one day true.

Planet of Terror

A monstrous sun rose, flaming over the distant horizon. Dawn was breaking on the sullen brooding planet of Phebol, well-known to all scientists and space-wayfarers as a planet of unspeakable horrors, of spine-crawling terror . . . and death.

A distant meteor streaked downwards and crashed amid a holocaust of flame and debris, shattering the awesome silence that had reigned since nightfall the previous day. The explosion was followed by a multitude of hoarse cries and ear-piercing screams, all betokening the fact that the planet was inhabited . . . but by what strange creatures? Four men from the planet known as Terra were to find out to their cost, before that mighty sun reached its zenith.

It was 09.37, Phebol time, when the Vogon assault erupted. It was an attack straight out of the text-books; short, sharp and destructive and almost totally effective. Almost but not quite.

The five Vogon ships materialized out of null-space under the huge Terran starship in strike formation. The leading aircraft hurtled up and over, attacking the topside control-bridge. The two outer craft peeled away to left and right, destroying the engines at the rear and forward

gunnery-bridge. The remaining two concentrated on the underside, sending searing ion-beams up at the vast bulk of the titanium-treated steel hull until it vapourized. The attack was over almost before it had begun. Moments later the great starship tore itself apart in a blinding flash that even dimmed the glare of the sun over Phebol.

In the leading assault-craft, the Vogon commander grinned. Three weeks before, the war-mad government of the planet of Vogos had decided on the outright destruction of Terra. Suspecting this, the Terrans had despatched a starship to reconnoitre Vogon airspace and report on any suspicious preparations. The starship had now fallen victim to a carefully arranged ambush before one word of a report on the attack could be relayed back to Terra.

The Vogon commander was rubbing his hands with mirth and triumph.

'That's one starship that won't be warning Terran Control of our intentions to . . .'

He was interrupted by one of his officers pointing suddenly to the main scanner-screen.

'L-look, Mighty One,' he stammered. 'Hurtling down into Phebol's atmosphere. It can't be debris.' His eyes widened. 'It's . . .'

'An escape-pod,' rasped the Vogon Commander. He reached out to touch a switch that would automatically sight a photon tracker-missile on the small plasti-glass domed craft but in that instant the escape-pod vanished into a swirling blue mass of banked cloud.

The commander bit his lips and smiled. 'Let the Terrans land on Phebol,' he chuckled. 'As we know full well, it's a planet of danger, of terrifying death. The Terrans will discover this. They will not survive its terrors.'

* * *

In the cramped interior of the escape-pod, Commander Nils Hardin of the Inter-Galactic Peace Patrol gazed grimly at the rapidly-approaching surface of the planet on the tiny scanner-screen in front of him. They were heading towards a desert of red soil and cruel rocks which stretched for miles.

For the third time Hardin punched out a corrective course on the small craft's control-console. For the third time, the computer failed to respond.

Hardin glanced at his three companions, George Rinker, the tall communications technician, and the two fitters Hugo Dorn and Heinie Garside. 'Better brace yourselves,' he said tersely. 'I managed to level off a few points before the computer flaked out. We're going to crash-land.'

All four adjusted their seat-belts and assumed the prescribed position to withstand the shock of a crash-landing.

'What hope?' Rinker managed to hiss.

'Little,' replied Hardin. 'The merest chance.'

He had scarcely uttered the words when the escape-pod crashed into a sea of sand, as insubstantial as a bed of feathers. Rocks and great gouts of sand were hurled in all directions and it seemed to the four Terrans as though their heads had been all but torn from their shoulders. Their senses reeled, blood trickled from their ears and all relapsed into a merciful unconsciousness.

* * *

Hardin awoke to find that Garside and Dorn were already on their feet. The floor of the small craft was littered with the wreckage of instruments and equipment, sundry jagged pieces of steel and alloy debris and shattered glass.

Nearby George Rinker was stirring painfully.

Hardin put his hand to a head that was pounding with pain.

'Vogons,' he muttered bitterly.

'Vogons?' repeated Garside, startled. 'What are you talking about?'

'Caught sight of their assault craft when I was struggling to alter our course after we ejected,' the commander explained.

'*What?*' shouted Garside. 'I thought the ships had simply . . . exploded. Just one of those fantastic space-stresses that suddenly occur and no-one's been able to work out why.'

'You think there were any other survivors?'

The three men looked at Rinker who was gazing blearily at Hardin. The commander grimaced.

'No', he replied. 'We're the only ones and if these two fitters hadn't been running a check on the nav-computer on this escape-pod and called you and me down to inspect it, we'd be so much fissionized dust floating around up there – like the rest of my crew.'

'What now?' asked Dorn.

'We get out,' said Hardin more crisply. 'The air in this pod won't last for more than an hour at most.' He glanced at the control-console and noted that the recycler had been smashed.

'Suit up,' he ordered.

It took half-an-hour to prepare to leave the craft. Pressure suits, laser-guns and suit radios had to be checked and rechecked and a supply of food-tabs was stowed by each man. Before the attack Hardin had taken a preliminary spectograph reading which showed that the atmosphere of Phebol, unknown to Terrans, contained a higher proportion of inert gases than an Earth-type world. The air would be breathable but suits would have to be worn.

The men left the escape-pod, their feet sinking deeply into the slush of sand. Garside had his laser-gun under his arm and pulled the trigger.

'Just making sure,' he grinned cockily as his three companions stared at him.

Curtly, Hardin motioned with a peremptory thumb. 'Get going,' he rapped out and Garside nodded, somewhat chastened.

The four men clumped through the feathery sand, Rinker striding beside his commander, Garside and Dorn trudging in their wake.

'I can't understand how we came to eject,' said Rinker frowning.

Hardin didn't bother to explain. A commander of the Inter-Galactic Patrol has to have razor-sharp reactions . . . must be able to take lightning-fast decisions in an emergency. Inside the escape-pod with the other three men he had felt the ship quiver at the first bombardment and had known instinctively that his craft was about to break up within micro-seconds. It was too late to do anything but jam his thumb over the vent button – which automatically sealed the tiny pod – slam down the ejector-bar . . . and hope for the best.

Now they were down. They had survived. But for how long. . . .?

They were millions of spacials from the nearest Terran-controlled planet, in an unexplored sector of the Galaxy. The planet they were on had not even been charted.

'There's a good chance that this planet is inhabited,' he said as he headed towards a narrow avenue between some towering rocks.

'Sure,' he heard Rinker reply. 'But if it is, at what level of technology are the natives? Will they have radio? Are we going to be able to contact the nearest Terran listening post?'

Hardin had no answer to these questions. Privately he doubted that the level of technology would be high, even if the planet were peopled at all. But there was no point in being pessimistic at this early stage.

The four men trudged on through the bleak world and as they headed into hilly country so the erstwhile foetid air became crisper. Hardin wondered if they would ever see Terra again. It seemed unlikely.

As they moved round a huge black-hued mesa, its rocky walls rearing high into the dark sky above them, Hardin suddenly stumbled and fell. His boots seemed to be wedged somehow. Muttering curses, he looked down and saw that his feet were caught in what seemed like strands of wafer-thin, gauzy tissue. But fragile as it looked, it was strong.

He pulled off a glove and tried to tear the stuff from his boots, grimacing as he touched it. It was tacky and stuck to his skin. He replaced the glove and turned and called to the others who were now a little way ahead.

'Hey! Come and give me a hand!'

The three men turned. Dorn suddenly uttered a horrified cry and pointed and at that moment, Hardin, staring over his houlder, saw something that seemed to freeze the blood in his veins.

At the bottom of the cliff, not fifty yards from where he was sitting was what looked to be, at first glance a huge spider. Hardin knew better than that.

He was looking at one of the deadliest creatures in the known Galaxy – a shell-backed arachnoid from the planet Saag.

The people of Saag trained them and used them in their unending wars as front-line combat weapons. The arachnoids sprayed a corrosive fluid from their huge beaks, a fluid that could penetrate steels while their razor-sharp pincers could rip a man apart in seconds. For all their bulk, they could move fast. As fast, in fact, as the monster that was even now scuttling towards the trapped Terran.

Hardin wrenched loose his laser-gun. More of the vile creatures were running down the side of the cliff, over an intricate network of steel-strong strands that made up their web. Sweating, Hardin, flipped over the safety-collar of the gun.

As he did so a spurt of fluid lanced through the air towards him. With his boots still snared in the gossamer-thin tissue, he could only roll his body and although this caused the stream of acid to over-shoot him, it also ruined his aim. He fired but the laser beam missed the arachnoid that continued onwards ever nearer. He severed long strands of the web, shattering the rock-face beyond.

The tremors caused by the blast on the cliff shook the other two arachnoids off and they hurtled to the ground, squealing with rage – a high-pitched ululation that set the hairs at the back of Hardin's neck bristling. Out of the corner of his eye, he saw Rinker fumbling desperately with a hand-laser but the comm-tec's first shot was a bad one.

Hardin snapped his helmet back over his face and fired again at the leading monster, now only yards away.

The laser-beam seared straight into the brute's gaping beak. The creature seemed to explode, bleeding chunks of flesh and fur and shell flying through the air and pattering down on to the rocks.

'Nail the other two!' Hardin yelled over his suit radio.

Rinker and Dorn were both using their lasers on the two remaining arachnoids who were now in retreat, scuttling back up the sagging web. Hardin wondered vaguely where Garside was and then sighted on the rear creature and fired for the third time. The arachnoid disappeared in a blaze of light.

'Got to get free of this stuff,' Hardin gasped, turning the laser-gun to low power. He triggered a short burst at the entangling tacky threads, which fell away from his boots and scrambled to his feet.

As he turned, he clenched his teeth in shock. Only feet away was all that remained of Garside. The acid the arachnoid had spat at him had hit the fitter.

He was aware of Rinker just behind him.

'Garside . . .?' began the comm-tec.

Hardin nodded briefly.

'We'll give him a decent burial.'

* * *

An hour later they were trudging on. All three men were still shaken by the day's events, and were now constantly looking about them,

always watching for fresh horrors.

'What I can't figure out,' Rinker was saying, 'is how the Vogons jumped us without our main sensors tagging them.'

'That's their prime secret,' said Hardin. 'That's where they beat us Terrans hand over fist. The only reason war hasn't been declared between our two races is that we've got more weapons than they have. But what they've got is in a way more important.'

'It's something to do with their starship engines, isn't it, sir?' said Dorn.

Hardin nodded.

'They use a type of mineral they call starfire quartz in their reactors. It enables them to move twice as fast as light itself. They can dematerialize at any given spot and within minutes materialize again millions of spacials from their original jumping-off point.'

'So why can't we mine this starfire quartz and use it ourselves?' asked Dorn.

Hardin smiled thinly.

'Because it's not to be found on any of the planets we've colonized. It's ultra-rare. Somewhere in the Galaxy the Vogons are mining the stuff and we can't even discover where it is.'

He threw himself down on to a bed of thick fronds and motioned to his companions to join him.

'Okay. Let's take a rest,' he said. Rinker and Dorn made themselves comfortable beside their commander.

'This is a nightmare planet,' muttered Rinker, baring his teeth. 'Those filthy arachnoids – what are they doing here? They belong on the planet Saag. And that's on the other side of the Galaxy!' He turned to Hardin. 'You're not going to tell me that life has evolved on this planet to include two totally different species of fauna?'

'I'm not going to tell you anything,' said Hardin grimly. 'I don't know how to explain it.'

Hugo Dorn suddenly pointed.

'Look there! Between those two rocks!'

They could see a plain stretching away to the horizon, consisting of what looked like red stubble dotted with bushes with drooping leprous-coloured fronds. Roaming across it was a herd of huge shaggy-haired beasts with leathery trunks and long, curling tusks. There were about a dozen of them, including three or four pups.

'Jagdars, from the planet Auroch,' muttered Rinker. 'And Auroch's millions of spacials from here.'

Hardin's eyes narrowed.

'Right! But no distance at all from Vogos!'

George Rinker frowned.

'I don't get it.'

Hardin smacked a gloved fist into the palm of his other hand, his face alight with excitement and realisation.

'Don't you see?' he rapped out. 'Saag . . . and now Auroch. Both planets in the Vogon sector of the Galaxy! And it was Vogon assault craft that jumped our ship! The Vogons have transported herds of vicious animals from their own planets to this one. They're patrolling the planet out there in space to keep Terran ships away. That's why our starship was destroyed. But if any craft does manage to get through, the crew are faced with the horrors of arachnoids and Jagdars.'

'If that's so, then you can bet your boots,' broke in Rinker, 'that there are other monstrous creatures all over this planet, all imported from Vogos itself or Vogon planets. A kind of insurance policy, just in case Terrans land here!'

'And that', added Dorn, 'adds up to the fact that they're trying to hide something. But what?' He looked at Hardin who shrugged.

'That's what we've got to find out.'

* * *

They found out three days later.

The three men stared over the lip of ground at the busy scene below. A wide natural valley stretched in front of them. A small makeshift township had been built to one side around vast smelting domes, near the cliff-face on their right, and smoke belched from tall chimneys, blackening the skies. Rails had been laid along the ground into caves in the cliffs, and carrier-pods ran back and forth from the caves to the factory area. Launch pads had been constructed on the left side of the valley, and the Terrans could see a variety of craft, including two massive starships, and a number of smaller fliers and planet-hoppers. At once the three men recognized the beings who swarmed about the township.

'Vogons!' muttered Rinker. 'And they're obviously mining. . . .'

'*Starfire quartz!*' Hardin snapped. 'It's got to be the answer! This planet supplies the Vogons with the mineral that enables their starships to move twice as fast as the speed of light! And that's why they don't want any Terrans snooping around! Somehow, we've got to get this information to Terra?'

He gestured at the launch area. 'We're going to have to steal one of their ships. A small flier'd do. All their craft are powered by the starfire reactor-drive.'

'And how d'you suggest we do that?' grunted Rinker.

Hardin turned and pointed back the way they'd come to where a herd of Jagdars were moving slowly across the layer of white gritstone that covered the ground.

'First of all, we stampede that herd through the narrow pass down there into the valley. That should cause enough confusion. The Vogon mining area's little more than a shanty-town. The Jagdars should trample it flat!'

They jogged back down the slope and moved towards the Jagdar herd. But Hardin had miscalculated. With their pressure-suits on, they felt no wind, but the massive beasts felt it – and smelt the newcomers' approach. Within seconds, they were charging towards the Terrans, trumpeting with rage. The dominant Jagdar – an enormous beast half as big again as the other animals – came thundering forward so fast that it drew ahead of the rest of the herd by at least four hundred yards. It bore down on Dorn.

'It'll pound us to a pulp!' gasped the fitter. 'Run for it!'

'Wait!' yelled Hardin. 'Don't move! Stay where you are!'

Waving his arms furiously, he dashed in front of the leading Jagdar then veered to one side. He had to force the Jagdar to head for the narrow pass into the valley of the Vogons beyond, and the only way to do that was to make it follow him, even at the risk of being crushed under its pounding feet.

Lungs burning, heart hammering, he sprinted towards the dark opening, followed by the enraged mammoth. At the last moment he sprang to one side, clinging on to a rock outcropping and hauling himself desperately upwards as the leading Jagdar thundered past him into the cutting. Unable to turn because of the narrowness of the pass, the mighty beast plunged on, followed by the rest of the herd, now a quarter of a mile behind their leader.

As Rinker and Dorn ran up, Hardin dropped back down to the ground. He flipped back his helmet-plate. In the distance they could hear the thunder of mighty feet, the shrill cries of the maddened herd, and the sharp hiss of laser-rifles.

Hardin jerked a thumb at the pass.

'We'd better move fast. We've got to reach the fliers before the Vogons wipe the brutes out.'

They ran through the pass and out into the valley. To their right, dust rose in a dense cloud, and they could vaguely make out the shapes of the giant beasts through the murk. Laser-bolts seared the air.

The nearest flier was sitting on a launch-pad only yards away from them. A Vogon suddenly spotted the running men and gave a yell, but Hardin flicked his hand-laser to low-power, fired, and the alien spun away. Seconds later the Terrans were inside the craft, and Hardin was punching out a take-off pattern into the computer.

* * *

Hunched over a console in the craft's cabin, Rinker was frowning at the keys in front of him. In the rear scanner-screen, the planet was receding from them at an acute angle.

'I've tapped out a Terran emergency signal,' said the comm-tec morosely, 'but who knows if anyone'll hear it.'

Hardin stared at the controls.

'And somehow I've got to figure out how to boost us into stardrive. Take-off and landing are okay, but the rest is guesswork.'

'Guess fast,' muttered Dorn. 'We've got five shadows – Vogon assault craft coming up fast!'

'Looks like this is it,' snapped Hardin. 'It's the planet patrol that jumped our starship. No way are we going to beat them off. I'll keep jinking, but . . .'

The five Vogons were converging on them. Any second, Hardin knew, their laser-batteries would open up.

And then he gasped – as, one after the other, the Vogon craft flared and exploded, brilliant flashes of light against the darkness of space.

A voice boomed over the speaker-system – a Terran voice.

'Not bad shooting, from over a thousand spacials away! I take it you're the Terrans who've just sent out an S.O.S.?'

'Commander Nils Hardin of the Inter-Galactic Patrol,' said Hardin crisply. 'My starship was destroyed by Vogons. It's a long story . . . .'

The voice laughed.

'Tell it when we pick you up. We happened to be near this sector of the Galaxy when contact was lost with your starship four days ago, and we were alerted. It's taken us that long to reach here.'

Hardin grinned.

'This time next year,' he said, 'that journey will take you four hours, not four days – once we start mining starfire quartz!'

Continued from page 85

Space Cadet

One day, soon after Jason January had been awarded a medal by the Director of Space Force I, a group of convicts from Earth were labouring on the airless surface of the moon. Under the watchful eyes of their guards they were loading a heavy truck with precious uranium ore. The moon had proved to be rich in uranium deposits.

One guard ordered the biggest prisoner to work harder, and, behind his space helmet, the former space pirate, Hercules Canute, scowled blackly.

In a sudden fit of rage, Hercules Canute seized the ball and chain fastened to his left ankle and hurled it at the truck full of ore. 'Share that among you!' he bellowed to the guards.

The mass of ore engulfed the unfortunate guards, and Canute shouted to the other convicts. 'Follow me!' he roared. 'Let's get away from this accursed moon!'

The convicts piled aboard a transport craft, and they were airborne before the guards recovered.

With Hercules Canute at the controls, the stolen craft came at last to a giant and long-deserted satellite that had been launched into an orbit between the Earth and the planet Venus by the Russians eight hundred years ago in the 21st Century.

Canute had used the satellite as a hideout when he operated as a pirate. Once inside, he ordered one of his companions to tune in the television. 'Let's see if they've heard of our escape on Earth,' he said.

Earth television could be received almost anywhere in the galaxy, and the escaped convicts were able to tune in to a programme from Paris. 'Greetings from the planet Earth,' began the announcer.

The announcer gestured to an assortment of space craft standing ready on their launch-pads. 'Today sees the start of the great Earth-to-Venus race,' he continued. 'Here we see craft from a variety of countries.'

The commentator's voice vibrated with sudden excitement. 'And here comes Great Britain's entry,' he cried. 'We are watching the arrival of the Royal Space Force craft!'

The British craft landed, and six trim figures in the uniforms of RSF cadets alighted. 'Here we see the crew,' cried the announcer. 'All are cadets of the Royal Space Force Academy, and their captain is Jason January.'

At the sight of Jason January and his companions, Hercules Canute turned purple. 'By the planets!' he thundered 'That's the young rogue who caused me to be captured and imprisoned!'

A few minutes later, Canute and the rest of the watching convicts on the desolate satellite saw the massed craft taking off for the hotly-contested race from Earth to distant Venus.

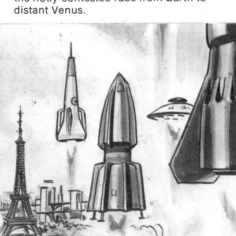

Clenching his gargantuan fists, Hercules Canute leapt to his feet and made a solemn and fearsome vow. . . .

'So Jason January is coming this way, eh?' he roared. 'Well, this is the chance I have been waiting for. I will destroy him, his craft . . . and his companions!'

Soon after Canute had made his threat, the RSF craft was passing through trackless space. Jason January ordered the class bully, Tom Bolt, to take over the controls. Knowing Bolt's character, Jason gave him firm instructions. 'Take good care to keep a close watch on everything,' he said.

Meanwhile, inside the ancient Russian space satellite, Canute and his ruffianly companions were gazing into the tele-radar. 'The craft taking part in the Earth-to-Venus race are now ten thousand miles distant,' gritted Hercules Canute. 'But they are heading this way. . . .'

Adjusting the tele-radar for a closer view of the oncoming craft, Canute saw something which brought a savage grin to his lips. 'The American craft is leading, followed by the RSF ship,' he cried. 'This gives me a great opportunity to get even with young Jason January.'

Still grinning, Canute pressed a switch. 'This radio brake was once used to stop any unmanned craft approaching the satellite,' he gloated, 'I shall stop the American craft in the path of January.'

Hopes of winning the race were running high in the leading American space-ship. The crew had realized that they were ahead of all their rivals. Suddenly, however, the engineer yelled with alarm. 'We're losing velocity, Skipper!' he shouted. 'The craft has almost stopped.'

Aboard the Royal Space Force craft, Tom Bolt was living up to his reputation for slacking on the job. Bored with a long spell at the controls, he had switched the ship on to automatic pilot, and, with his eyes closed was listening to a transistor radio.

Some sixth sense of impending doom aroused Jason from his slumber. He opened his eyes and sat up with a start, just in time to see the rear end of the American craft looming up close ahead. 'Wake up, Bolt! Look alive, you lazy bonehead!' he shouted. 'Use your starboard reactors. It's our only chance.'

Bolt obeyed Jason's order . . . but too late. Veering to one side, the Royal Space Craft struck the stationary American ship a glancing blow, ripping the rear end from the American craft.

Jason's craft was soon out of sight. The American captain was quick to act. He gave the order to abandon ship . . . and the control compartment was propelled from the wrecked hull, only a few seconds before the atomic power plant of the vessel blew up with a terrifying roar.

Drifting in the airless waste, with no chance of returning to Earth, the American crew were in a desperate plight. Then they saw the ancient satellite looming out of the darkness ahead of them.

Hoping against hope that the old satellite was habitable, the Americans brought their escape capsule alongside, and clawed their way aboard in their pressure suits.

Once inside the airlock, they came face to face with Hercules Canute. 'Good day, gentlemen,' leered the space pirate, aiming his gun at the newcomers. 'You are now my prisoners. If you know what's good for you, put up your hands.'

Meanwhile, aboard the Royal Space Force craft, Jason January and his cadets were quite unaware of the predicament of the Americans. They radioed news of the disaster back to Earth . . . and waited with troubled hearts to hear what had happened to the American crew.

The reply, when it came, was terse: 'You will immediately abandon all further participation in the race, and return to Earth at once in order to face charges of criminal negligence!'

Jason January and his comrades realized that they were in dire trouble. Their old enemy, Hercules Canute, seemed to have succeeded in revenging himself.

Within the space of a few hours, horrified crowds who had gathered in Times Square, New York, were staring at the report of the disaster. They filed past, gazing up at the announcement in grief.

The American President addressed the nation over a coast-to-coast television hook-up. 'Nothing can restore our lost heroes to their families and loved ones,' he said, sternly. 'But I shall demand compensation from the British Government for this act of negligence.'

The British Cabinet was summoned to an all-night meeting to discuss the grave situation. 'This incident could ruin Anglo-American unity and friendship for many years to come,' said the Prime Minister.

Meanwhile, the cause of the sensation was descending on its landing pad at the Royal Space Force Academy at Portsmouth. And an armed guard awaited Jason January and his crew.

As soon as Jason and his companions stepped out of their ship, they were put under close arrest by the guards and led to the quarters where they were to be confined.

Anxious to impress the Americans, the Royal Space Force court-martialled Jason and his crew the very next day. 'You claim that the American craft stopped dead in mid-space,' snapped the prosecuting officer to Jason. 'Even if that claim proved to be true, why did you not turn aside from it?'

Jason cast a sideways glance at Tom Bolt, the class bully, whose carelessness had caused the collision. But Jason was the craft's captain. 'I have no excuse, sir,' he said. 'I accept full responsibility.'

The verdict was a foregone conclusion. 'Cadet Jason January,' said the judge. 'You are dismissed from the Royal Space Force. Your crew are exonerated from all blame!'

And so, on the parade ground of the Royal Space Force Academy which he loved so dearly, Jason January was subjected to the full disgrace of public dismissal. In front of his comrades, he was stripped of his badges, buttons and ceremonial dagger.

Far away in space . . . in the ancient satellite . . . Canute watched Jason's downfall on the TV screen and chuckled with delight. 'That settles my account with him. Moreover, I have a money-making idea.'

Two weeks later, the weekly space-liner from Earth to Venus was hurtling at supersonic speed through the vast emptiness of space. All was quiet and serene in the luxuriously-appointed first class compartment as silent-footed and efficient hostesses served the wealthy passengers with the choicest and most succulent foods that Earth could provide.

Midway to Venus, the space-liner's navigator noted the long-deserted Russian satellite some way ahead. Then to his utter astonishment, the gigantic craft in which he was travelling seemed to stop dead as if grasped by an invisible hand.

While the startled passengers milled about in fear and confusion, panic reigned in the control compartment of the liner. 'What stopped us? I can't understand it.' cried the chief engineer. Outside, space-suited figures swarmed about the liner.

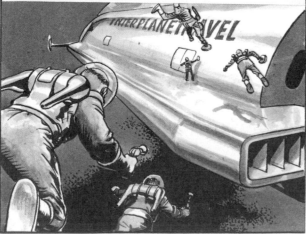

Presently, the airlock door swung open . . . and Hercules Canute strode into the first class compartment. 'Good day. ladies and gentlemen,' he sneered. 'Raise your hands above your head . . . and look lively about it!'

The wealthy passengers in the first class lounge were dumbfounded when they realized that they were being robbed in mid-space on a flight from Earth to Venus. Eagerly, Canute's pirates collected wallets, rings, watches and jewellery of every description. Completely cowed by the raiders' guns none of the travellers offered the slightest resistance.

'My plan is fool-proof,' Canute gloated. 'After the robbery, this liner will just disappear and no one will be any the wiser.'

Deprived of their valuables, the dismayed passengers found themselves being herded from the space liner into the satellite which had by now docked alongside.

'We've room for hundreds of prisoners inside this old satellite,' boomed Canute. 'Later on, we'll be able to ransom each and every one of them for every penny they own.'

Drifting off, the satellite blew up the liner by remote control.

But Canute was not content with one hi-jacking. Within another month, he struck twice more. All Earth knew was that three craft had vanished.

At about that time, the Ranger class at the Royal Space Academy were called together by their chief instructor, the respected Wing-Commander Paddy Keane. 'We leave tomorrow for Venus . . . for a course of training in special deep-space techniques,' he announced.

Next morning, Wing-Commander Keane led his class of cadets aboard the giant space liner which was to transport them to the distant planet of Venus. At the top of the gangway, the whole Ranger class gasped with astonishment. Waiting to greet them, dressed in a steward's white jacket and black trousers, was none other than . . . Jason January!

'What are you doing here, Jason?' gasped Nick. Jason hung his head. 'With my record, I couldn't get a better job,' he answered.

Soon after, the space liner soared up into the sky and set course for its far-distant destination . . . the planet Venus.

Tom Bolt, the class bully, had been responsible for allowing Jason's craft to be involved in the fateful collision for which Jason had taken the blame. But there was no gratitude in Bolt's mean heart. 'That bighead has got his just desserts,' thought Bolt. 'It serves him right. I'm going to rub his nose in it while I've got the chance!'

As Jason January came along the gangway, intent on his menial task of carrying a laden tray, Tom Bolt stuck out his foot. Jason tripped and fell, sending two cups of hot coffee hurtling on to the bald head of an irate passenger. 'Ha, ha! What a clumsy clot that steward is,' crackled Bolt.

Jason turned upon the class bully, his face flushed with fury. 'That was no accident, Bolt!' he snapped. Tom Bolt grinned, tauntingly. 'Well! So what are you going to do about it?' he sneered.

Jason January snatched up a large and sloppy ice-cream pudding from a nearby trolley. 'This is what I'm going to do about it, Bolt, my friend,' he rasped. And, with these words, he thrust the pudding straight into the bully's sneering face.

The chief steward came running to the scene. 'I saw that,' he shouted at Jason. 'You deliberately assaulted that passenger. You're sacked . . . do you hear me . . . sacked! And, if I have anything to do with it, I'll see that you never get another job aboard a space liner again!'

Jason's lips tightened as he met the chief steward's angry gaze. Having already blighted his career, it seemed that Bolt had now got him sacked from his job.

As he stood facing the enraged chief steward, Jason January little knew that the space liner was now passing the ancient Russian satellite which had first provided Canute with a refuge, and which now served as a prison for his captives.

Inside the satellite, Hercules Canute sat at the control panel of the equipment that was once used for stopping unmanned craft. 'Stand by for action!' he commanded.

Aboard the space liner, assistant steward Jason January had lost all control of his temper. 'Go and fry your face, you insignificant little shrimp!' he shouted at the chief steward. 'Pompous people give me a pain in the neck! You needn't sack me, chum . . . I resign!'

Back on the satellite Canute pressed the button, and the space liner came to a stop with a shuddering jolt. The passengers' attention had been fixed on the fracas in the gangway, but they forgot all about it when they were sent flying from their seats.

Jason picked himself up. He had landed on the chest of Tom Bolt, the class bully. 'What on earth could have happened?' cried the ex-captain of the cadets. 'What made the space liner stop in mid-air like that?'

A hundred yards away from the now-stationary space ship lurked the dark shape of the sinister satellite. The space-suited figures of Canute and his men emerged from its bulk. Miniature jets in their suits propelled them towards the helpless space liner.

Minutes later, the passengers aboard the space liner gasped when Hercules Canute lifted his space helmet from his bullet head. 'It's just like the highwaymen of olden times,' he guffawed. 'Don't be alarmed. All I want is your money . . . or your lives!'

Then Jason and Canute came face to face. 'What have we here?' hissed the space pirate. 'If it isn't the daring young cadet who had me and my men sent to prison!'

Canute noticed Jason's white coat. 'Oh, so you're not a space cadet any more,' he sneered. 'My hi-jacking operation got you dismissed from the Space Force, eh?' Jason realized Canute had caused the collision.

A curt order from Canute, and the passengers were transferred to the satellite. 'Take special care of the Royal Space Force gentlemen,' boomed the space pirate.

Jason and the cadets were placed in a dark compartment that had once been the living quarters of the Russian crew of the old satellite. It was there that Nick Ringold made a surprising discovery. 'Hey, Jason! Look what I've found!' he exclaimed.

Meanwhile, the space pirates were gorging themselves on the rich food they had stolen from the space liner. 'The grub is not bad, but I won't be happy until we've left this old hulk,' grunted one. 'There's something about it that fair gives me the creeps!'

'Enough of that talk,' snapped Canute, contemptuously. 'Next you'll be telling me that you've seen the ghosts of the ancient Russians who lived here more than five hundred years ago.'

One of the pirates raised a shaking finger. 'Look, Canute!' he faltered.

Out of the gloom flitted two fearsome figures clad in the space-suits which Russian cosmonauts had used many centuries ago. The pirates gazed at the two spectral forms which glowed with a ghostly light.

'The ghosts of the ancient Russian cosmonauts,' gasped one of the space pirates. 'They've come back to warn us to keep away.'

Appearing to shimmer with a weird and unearthly glow, the two apparitions closed in on the group of pirates. 'It's a warning to us,' gasped one of Canute's men. 'They don't want us here. They don't care for human company!'

'Niet!' the Russian word for 'No', burst from one of the strange figures. This was more than sufficient for the scared pirates. They turned and fled, ignoring their brutal leader's harsh order: 'Come back here, you bunch of spineless swabs!'

The craft which they had stolen from the Moon, in which they had first travelled to the old satellite, lay beside the air lock. The pirates swarmed aboard.

Within seconds, the frightened pirates had manoeuvred the Moon craft through the air lock and were hurtling away from the ancient Russian satellite. Soon, they had disappeared into the trackless wastes of space.

The gigantic Hercules Canute was left all alone to face the 'ghosts'. He gave vent to a snarl of utter fury as they removed their old-style space helmets . . . to disclose the grinning faces of Jason January and Nick Ringold. 'You two!' barked Canute. 'I might have known it!'

'We found these old suits and escaped from the compartment through a ventilator,' said Jason. 'Lashings of luminous paint completed the illusion!'

The space pirate's massive hand flashed to the pistol at his belt. But Jason re-acted with lightning speed. As Canute drew, he leapt forward . . . and the burning flash of the disintegrating bolt missed the back of the cadet's head by mere inches.

But the searing blast of the burly pirate's weapon utterly destroyed the bank of radio gear behind Jason January.

Jason and Nick stared at the damage in dismay, but Hercules Canute roared with diabolical glee. 'You've done it now,' he boomed. 'You'll never get a message through to Earth. We'll be stuck here for all eternity!'

The released prisoners held a council of war and it was Wing-Commander Paddy Keane who came up with the solution. 'We'll have to get the propulsion rockets working on this old hulk,' he said. 'Somehow, we must fly her back to Earth.'

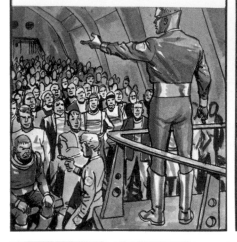

The ancient motors were plastered with the grime and rust of eight centuries, and Hercules Canute was given the job of cleaning them. 'Stop glaring at me and get on with the job, Hercules,' laughed Jason, 'I warn you that you'll get no supper until I can see my face reflected in that shining metal like a mirror.'

Two days later, the great moment came. At an order from Wingco Keane, the ancient rocket engines were fired for the first time in ages. With a jerk, the old satellite moved out of its present orbit and turned its nose towards distant Earth.

Then . . . just when everyone aboard was cheering . . . the sound of the rockets died. 'Great Scott!' cried Wingco Keane. 'If we can't get them going again, we'll never be able to steer this thing.'

Twelve hours later, a strange planet came into their vision. 'Stand by for a crash landing,' shouted Keane. 'Make sure you strap yourselves in. We're in for a nasty crunch.'

Lacking any propulsive power, Paddy Keane was unable to check the old craft's speed or change its course. With a resounding splash, the satellite dropped into what appeared to be a lake.

But, in reality, they had come down in a puddle at the feet of two young boys. The strange planet was populated by giants.

110

It took Jason and his companions some time to recover from the spine-jarring impact of the satellite striking the surface of the water. When they had struggled to their feet, Tom Bolt pointed a trembling finger at the observation window. 'What's that peering in at us?' he cried. 'It looks like a giant eye!'

One of the boys who had found the satellite was built on a scale so large that he was able to pick up the old space craft just like a toy. Together with his friend, he hurried towards a city whose buildings were constructed in weird and fantastic shapes.

Entering a building which housed a large laboratory, the boys eagerly showed their find to a group of scientists. The scientists placed the satellite on a table and gazed at it in puzzlement. 'What a strange object,' said one.

Under the pressure of one of the giant's fingers, the air lock door slid open. 'Follow me, lads,' cried Wingco Keane. 'Let's get out and find just where we are.' Cowardly Tom Bolt drew back. 'I'm not going out there. It may be dangerous!' he wailed.

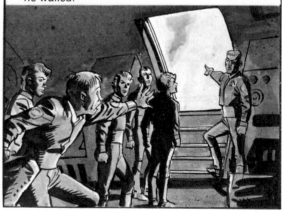

Keane repeated his order sternly, and Bolt joined the cadets and the convicts as they filed out of the satellite. They looked up . . . to see a group of enormous faces staring solemnly down at them.

But the cowardly bully did not get very far. A giant finger and thumb plucked him upwards.

One by one, like so many toy soldiers, the cadets and the convicts were picked up by the chief scientist and lowered gently into a large and ornately-carved box. They were quite helpless.

Tom Bolt's nerve broke. With a panic-stricken cry, he raced down to the table-top.

Carrying their diminutive captives in the box, the scientists made their way across the city towards a fabulous building . . . the palace of their ruler.

The ruler of the city was a spoilt and sullen boy whose savage temper and sudden rages were feared by all his subjects. When he beheld the tiny prisoners, however, the boy king's eyes lit up with interest and sheer child-like delight.

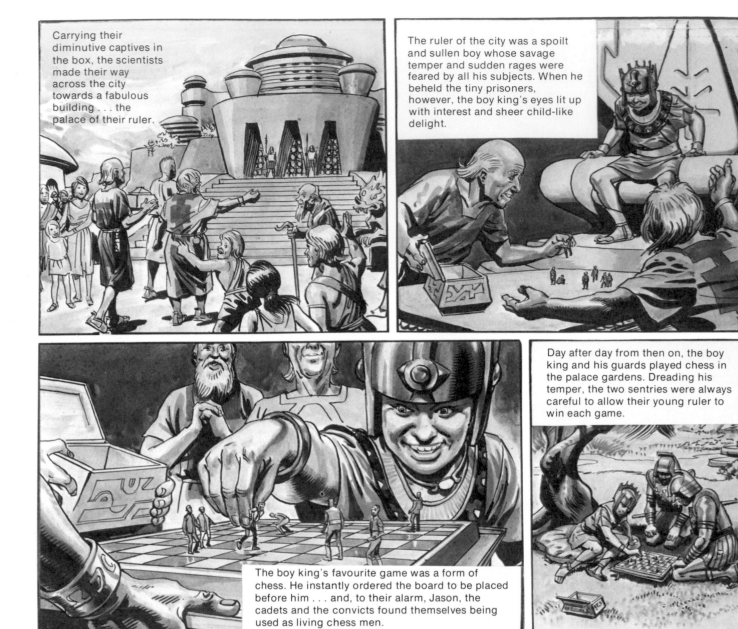

Day after day from then on, the boy king and his guards played chess in the palace gardens. Dreading his temper, the two sentries were always careful to allow their young ruler to win each game.

The boy king's favourite game was a form of chess. He instantly ordered the board to be placed before him . . . and, to their alarm, Jason, the cadets and the convicts found themselves being used as living chess men.

One day, after an arduous game in the hot sun, the chess men were returned to their box. It was then that Jason made a momentous decision. 'I've had enough of playing games,' he cried. 'Give me a leg up, someone. I'm getting out of here!'

Jason peered cautiously over the top of the box, and saw that the boy king and his guards were sound asleep in the sunshine. He saw something else, too. A giant spider was descending towards the sleeping boy, its jaws agape to inflict a poisonous bite.

Jason climbed out of the box followed by Canute, who grabbed him by the arm. 'Let the spider bite him,' snarled the pirate. 'That brat deserves everything he gets!'

Hercules Canute was a massive and immensely strong opponent, but Jason January had trained for years to become adept at judo. Seizing the space pirate in a deft arm-lock, he sent him hurtling through the air to land flat on his back.

As Canute bellowed with rage, Jason snatched up a twig which to him was a stout branch. Fearlessly, he fended off the spider. Awakened by Hercules Canute's yell, the young king and the two sentries saw what was happening.

'This little fellow saved your life, your majesty,' said one of the guards, as he speedily dispatched the spider. The boy king peered at Jason. 'So he did,' he agreed. 'That was brave. He shall be suitably rewarded.'

Jason and Canute were returned to the box. 'You young dunder-head,' rasped the pirate. 'Why didn't you let the spider settle that giant brat's hash? We'd have had one less enemy then.'

Early next day, Jason learned what form his reward was to take. Carefully lifted out of the box by giant, but gentle hands, he was placed on a table on top of a spool of tailor's thread. Then he was measured for a new suit of clothes.

Dressed in a miniature version of the uniform of the Royal Guards, Jason was made to stand on the table while the young king scoffed enormous meals.

Having picked up the language of the giants, Jason learnt that they feared attack from a country called Yargon. 'They destroy all our reconnaissance craft,' said an officer.

'Why don't you use us?' yelled Jason at the top of his voice. 'We could gather information over Yargon. Our satellite would be too small to be picked up by their radar.'

And he added, almost as an afterthought: 'But you would have to give us a hand to put our satellite back in flying order.'

'We agree to your suggestion,' replied the young king. 'Our scientists will repair your craft immediately.'

The scientists set to work to put the satellite in order. 'It's a fiddling task,' muttered one. 'But we'll soon do it.'

Working in shifts by day and night the young ruler's scientists eventually had the craft ready for blast-off, perched on the top of a special rocket they had constructed. 'All aboard!' cried Wingco Keane.

On the following day, the great moment came. The rocket, with the satellite on top, was set up in a container of sand in the palace gardens. The boy king and his officers cheered as the control-button was pressed and the rocket and satellite rose high in the air on a tail of flame.

Once free of the planet's gravitational pull, the satellite separated from the rocket. 'That's the first stage completed,' said Paddy Keane, as he sat at the controls. 'Our next task is to proceed to Yargon. Study the charts the king gave us, navigator, and plot the necessary course.'

Then Hercules Canute took a hand in the proceedings. 'Forget it,' he rasped, drawing his gun. 'I've got my own plans for this satellite, and they don't include doing anything to help those overgrown swabs we've just left behind us.'

114

Canute stood at the rear of the control cabin, his deadly disintegrater aimed at Wing-Commander Paddy Keane and the young cadets. 'Set course for Jupiter,' he commanded. 'I've got friends there . . . space pirates like myself.'

Jason noticed that the pirate was standing on a metal plate let into the fibre of the deck. This gave him an idea. With his hands behind his back, he cautiously unplugged a live electric lead.

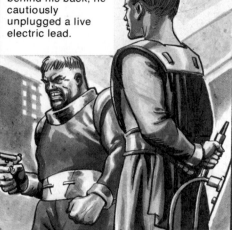

Jason January tossed the end of the lead on to the metal plate and a shower of sparks shot into the air as contact was made. The powerful current surged through Canute's body and he found himself doing a war dance.

When he calculated that Canute was ready to give in, Jason switched off the current. The space pirate sank to the deck and Wingco Keane turned back to the control panel. 'Right!' Set course for Yargon,' he ordered.

Its engines roaring as if they were brand-new, the ancient satellite orbited the strange planet.

Soon, Jason checked the charts and reported to the Wing-Commander that the craft was fast approaching the territory occupied by the warlike Yargon nation. Keane switched on the tele-radar and peered at what was revealed upon the screen.

As the focus sharpened, the Wing-Commander and his cadets saw row upon row of sleek and deadly space-fighters lined up on the ground beneath them. 'Yargon is obviously ready to attack our allies,' snapped Keane. 'We must pass on this information so that they can take counter-measures.'

115

As the only member of the crew who could speak the language, Jason reported the news of the impending Yargon attack to the young king and his officers over the satellite's radio.

'The boy king thanks us,' said Jason to the others. 'He wishes us a speedy and safe return to our own planet, Earth.'

And so it was that, many solar days later, the ancient Russian satellite powered itself across space and soared back into Earth's orbit for the first time in eight centuries.

Keane had radioed news of their arrival ahead of them, and a great multitude of people watched as the old craft descended on to the landing pad at Portsmouth.

All over the world, people sat glued to their TV screens. 'The mystery of the missing space liners is solved,' came the announcement. 'All thanks to Jason January and his comrades!'

'This is Hercules Canute,' continued the commentator. 'He was responsible for the space race collision and for the hi-jacked liners.'

The proudest moment of Jason January's life came a few days later. Standing on the parade ground of the academy at Portsmouth and watched by his cheering friends, he was restored to his rank as Captain of Cadets and was decorated by the same man who had dismissed him in disgrace only months earlier . . . the Marshal of the Royal Space Force.

Eye in Orbit

Astronomers studying the planets and other bodies in outer space were, across many years, handicapped by one difficult problem. This was the fact that the thick fuzzy blanket of the Earth's atmosphere gave them an indistinct view of the heavenly bodies.

Even observatories on high ground in areas where the climate offers clear night skies are not free from this shortcoming.

However, with rockets boosting all kinds of satellites into space, it was obviously a good idea to put a telescope into orbit outside the haze of the Earth's atmosphere and operate it by remote control so that a camera attached to it could take photographs.

America made their first attempt with what they called an OAO – an orbiting astronomical observatory. The rocket used to launch this failed and the OAO did not get into orbit. A second one was launched on 7th December 1968. To the delight of astronomers everywhere, it was an outstanding success.

Dome of Doom

The slim, streamlined spacer thrust smoothly through the deep black void of outer space. Lights blazed from the plasti-reinforced glass dome that covered the control cabin and, inside, figures could be seen moving about.

Far off by millions of miles, the home Galaxy sprawled across the sky like a gigantic spiral of light. The spacer flashed past a small group of nearby planets, hazy shimmering balls of red, green, orange and white.

Tired eyes watched a monitored close-up inside the control cabin.

'Another hour at Warp 14, Captain, and we should be there.'

'O.K., Slim, you might as well snatch a forty-five. We'll give you a shout when we need you.'

Navigator Slim Hewitt yawned hugely and patted his gaping mouth. He stood up and stretched his arms.

'Thanks, Captain – I need it! Forty-five minutes worth of complete relaxation will make a new man of me. Five hours in that navigating chair and I'm just about bushed.'

Captain Jack Weston gazed after his Chief Navigator as he strode from the control room. He turned to the spry little Scotsman who stood by a massive array of dials on the main instrument panel.

'Old Slim could do with a few months leave, Grant,' said Jack. 'He's getting the yawns – been on Outer Space patrol too long. It could be fatal in an emergency.'

'I wouldn't argue with ye, Captain,' grunted Grant Fraser, the pugnacious little Scots engineer. 'I could do with two or three months in Glasgow myself.'

'You'd get yourself into so many punch-ups you'd need another month in hospital,' grinned Jack. 'I know you, Grant. The only way you can keep out of trouble is to stay cooped up in a space-ship.'

The three men, together with Radio Operator Mike Conway and Ensign Colin Hughes, had been on routine patrol in Outer Space for three months. Now it was back to Earth to make their report to General Carstairs, chief of Space Operations.

But Jack had decided to make a short stop-over at the Earth Colony on the Moon. One of the spacer's emergency retro-rockets had developed a minor fault and, although the emergency rockets were rarely used, it was, reasoned Jack,

better to be safe than sorry, and the two repair centres on the Moon were manned by skilled technicians.

'Can't understand it, Captain . . .!'

Jack glanced round at the tough-looking black-bearded man who had just entered the cabin. He was bluff and bulky, and an old-fashioned bulldog pipe protruded from the breast pocket of his overalls.

'What's the trouble, Mike?'

'It's the radio. Can't seem to get a peep out of Lunar Control. The whole works seem to have blanked out.'

Radio Operator Mike Conway was one of the best communications experts in the Space Corps, and was a comrade of Jack's of long standing. He pulled the blackened pipe from his pocket and rammed it between his teeth.

Jack glanced at the monitor in front of him. At the incredible speed at which they were travelling, he knew that the Moon would be filling the video-screen in little less than an hour.

'That's very odd,' he muttered. 'As far as I know, there's nothing very special going on there at the moment, so it can't be a security blanket.' He glanced round the cabin at the men watching him anxiously. 'Anyone got any ideas?'

Mike Conway shook his head.

'Not a thing, Jack. There are only four stations on the Moon – the maximum security prison on the dark side, the two repair-and-fuelling centres, and the research station.'

'What about the research station?'

The speaker was Ensign Hughes, a boy in his late teens with a mop of curly black hair which no comb could keep tidy.

'Nothing there, Colin,' said Jack. 'There's no secret about what's going on there – they're just experimenting with food-growths, trying to see if some sort of vegetation can be produced in an airless atmosphere.'

'Sounds nutty to me,' murmured Colin, recently a cadet at a space college and now a member of Jack's team. 'I mean, how can you grow plants with no air? It's impossible.'

'I thought you'd passed through college with flying colours,' said Mike. 'You should know that they've been experimenting with artificial growths for years now – subjecting plant-life to concentrated gamma rays and atomic dust.'

'The scientists reckon that they can now grow

food just about anywhere,' Jack went on. 'The best place to test the theory is on an airless asteroid like the Moon. If they can cultivate plant-life on that, the food problems of the whole Galaxy will be solved in no time.'

'So, like you said, Jack – there's no secret there that anybody would want to steal,' said Mike. 'And, in any case, we've probably got hold of the wrong end of the stick. We're all presuming that the Moon's under attack, or something. There could be a dozen reasons why we can't get through to them by radio.'

'Sure,' said Colin. 'Could be a mammoth power failure.'

Grant Fraser, the little Scot, shook his head.

'Not on the Moon, laddie,' he replied. 'I happen to know that they've got four emergency power plants set up there. They can't all have broken down at the same time – plus the main supply.'

Jack eyed his companions and then grinned mischievously.

'Of course, we could get into touch with headquarters and pass the whole thing over to them,' he mused. 'But we've had a dull and boring patrol and I think we're entitled to a little excitement. We'll look into this matter ourselves.

Mind you, if we make a mess of it, General Carstairs will have my skin. But that's my affair, and I'm willing to take the risk!'

Shortly less than an hour later, the slim spacer hovered bird-like over the main touchdown pad on Lunar Repair Centre Unit 1, its retro-rockets hissing gently. And then, slowly, the great bulk gently lowered itself until it finally came to rest on the vast ferro concrete floor.

Then the main door hissed open, the lift cage slid out and down, and Jack and his companions stepped on to the Moon's dusty surface.

Ahead of them lay the squat bunker that led to the repair personnel headquarters. Normally lights would have blazed from its windows, and recovery vehicles would be skimming across the flat surface towards them.

But now no light showed, and the launch pad was devoid of any sort of activity. Its very stillness had a sinister, doom-laden quality about it.

'You were right, Jack,' Mike Conway's voice crackled inside Jack Weston's space-helmet. 'Not a sign of anyone. Something's up!'

'Better be ready for anything, men,' said Jack. 'Colin, you go with Mike to the repair personnel blockhouse main door. Grant, you come with me. We'll take a snoop around the outside.'

The four men split up. Jack watched Colin and Mike move towards the blockhouse, and then he signalled to Grant.

Ahead of them lay the huge stone dome which housed the various laboratories used by the research scientists. The two men walked slowly towards it.

Nothing stirred. No movement attracted their attention, either beside the dome or on the wide craggy plateau on which it rested.

'Captain!' Grant's voice broke through the thick silence inside Jack's helmet. 'The air-lock door. Look – it's open!'

'You're dead right, Grant,' snapped Jack. 'And the first rule of living on airless planets is: always close an airlock door after you! Come on, we'd better see what's going on inside.'

They entered the building and closed the door behind them.

They walked side-by-side down the corridor, the sound of their boots echoing away into the eerie stillness.

At the end was a door. Grant pushed at it, and it swung open. The little Scot gave a gasp of shocked surprise.

The room in front of them was a shambles. Furniture lay everywhere, smashed to pieces. Cushions and curtains and other fabrics had

been ripped to shreds and strewn all over the floor. Pictures had been torn from the walls and shards of glass were scattered where the frames had been thrown. And a man was lying amid the debris, still and silent, with a terrible gash across his forehead!

'He's alive, Captain,' muttered Grant. 'Look! He's opening his eyes!'

The man's eyelids fluttered, then opened fully. His eyes registered recognition when he saw Jack.

'Captain Weston!' The voice was low and hoarse. 'Th-thank heavens you've arrived. There's been trouble . . . big trouble. The convicts from the prison colony . . . they've escaped and run riot over the whole of the Moon centre.'

The man struggled to rise, but Jack pressed him back to the floor and pushed what was left of a cushion under his head.

'O.K., old chap, take it easy for a moment. You've had a nasty knock. We'll deal with this.'

Still the wounded man tried to rise. His eyes blurred over and specks of saliva bubbled at the corners of his mouth.

'But you don't understand,' he gasped. 'There's more . . . the convicts don't know . . . it's the weed! The weed that . . .' His voice faded, and his head flopped back on the cushion.

'I'd like to get my hands on whoever gave him that clout across the head!' snarled Grant. 'But what did he mean about the weed?'

'I don't know, Grant. He was probably rambling. He's passed out again, anyway. Come on.' Jack got to his feet. 'We'd better contact Mike and Colin, and get back to the ship. We should be able to sort out this little lot in no time. They can't have many weapons.'

'On the contrary, Weston – we've got plenty of weapons!'

Jack whipped round at this unexpected interruption.

In the doorway stood two villainous-looking thugs in convict garb, black nylon boiler-suits and heavy boots. Both were armed with Police Positives, ray-blasters that could cut a man in half!

Jack gasped as he recognized the cruel scarred features of the speaker.

'Varlag – the Solon space pirate! I might have known you'd have something to do with this!'

The Solon grinned evilly.

'Sure! I got sick of prison life, and there hasn't been a break-out on Moon colony for years. The guards were lax, easy to over-power. Me and my buddy Neilson here . . .' he gestured to his companion, a well-known Earth renegade who had sided with the Solons in the Great Space War years before . . . 'reckon we can use this dump as our headquarters for a few . . . er . . . projects we have in mind.'

'You won't get away with this,' grated Grant Fraser.

'Think not? I shouldn't be too sure about that,' sneered the Solon. 'We've already captured your pals – and taken over your spacer. I reckon we've got things very nicely tied up indeed!'

Quickly, Jack and Grant were hustled into a huge hall, where, normally the research scientists would take their meals. Now the room was filled with shouting swaggering convicts who were eating and drinking their fill of whatever they could grab. The din was indescribable.

At one end, Mike and Colin and a few of the space boffins had been herded together under the watchful eyes of a small group of convicts all of whom were armed to the teeth.

'Move it, Weston!' snarled Varlag. 'Join your pals while you can. You won't spend much time together, believe me.'

Neilson cackled with laughter. It was an ugly sound.

'That's right!' he sniggered. 'And I'll tell you for why. You're a dead lumber to us, the lot of you. So we're going to finish you all off.'

A cold finger touched Jack's spine. He knew these stir-crazy convicts. They had nothing to lose, since most of them were in for life anyway. He knew that Neilson meant what he said.

'Sorry, Captain – they jumped us as we entered the refuelling block. Didn't stand a chance.' Mike Conway's expression was bitter. He moved closer to Jack. 'It doesn't matter about us . . . it's the kid I'm worried about!'

'All right, you mugs . . . shaddup!' It was Varlag, yelling through a loud-hailer at the milling mob of roistering convicts. 'We'll move these space types up, and then we can start organising the place.'

Eager hands grasped at Jack and his men and thrust them into a tight bunch in one corner of the room.

Neilson ambled forward, a ray-blaster gripped professionally in one hand.

'I reckon I could cut you into tiny bits all by myself,' he grinned. He raised the gun and aimed it straight at Jack. 'Let's see if I can!'

SSSPPZZAAAAAKK!

A blaster-bolt seared the air and exploded on the floor with the noise of a piano being dropped from a sixth-floor window.

But it didn't come from Neilson!

'Uhh!' The convict turned in surprise – and Jack Weston leapt at him.

Neilson twisted, but he was too late. A fist like a lump of rock thudded against his jaw and he dropped senseless to the floor. Jack grabbed the gun and fired it over the heads of the startled convicts.

'Get back!' he snapped. 'I'll drop the first man who moves!'

'But who . . .?' Grant looked around him in amazement.

And then a figure emerged from the shadows and joined the little group.

'Slim! Slim Hewitt!' gasped Jack. 'Heck, of course! It had to be you!'

Slim Hewitt grinned.

'Sure! No-one remembered to wake me up when I went for a rest, and the first thing I knew was when the convicts took over the ship. But they were too slow. I hid in a bulkhead and waited till the coast was clear. Then I grabbed a gun and followed them.'

'You got here in the nick of time, chum,' said Mike Conway. 'I think . . .' But what Mike thought was lost, as the screaming voice of Varlag echoed round the room.

'You haven't won yet, Weston, curse you! You've got two guns – we've got a hundred and two. You haven't a hope!'

Angry murmurings filled the chamber. The rest of the convicts had recovered from their shock. A few of the more courageous edged closer to the little group round Jack.

Jack signalled to his navigator and raised his gun.

And then it happened!

The opposite wall was smashed apart as if a giant hand had plunged through it – and through the gap came a writhing mass of monstrous green tentacles.

Slowly, the tentacles groped about. Then one slid over Varlag's fallen body, grabbed it – and lifted the horrified convict into the air. Varlag let out a wild scream of terror.

'Suffering Saturn!' gasped Jack. 'In heaven's name what is it?'

The weight of the wriggling green mass pushed at what was left of the wall. The remaining buckled and sagged. Then, with a rending noise and in a cloud of dust and brick particles, the whole wall collapsed on to the panic-stricken mob of convicts. Varlag was dashed to the floor as if he were a rag doll.

The air was filled with dust and flying debris and the animal sounds of frightened screaming men. The huge mass of green shuddered and squirmed and then slowly heaved itself over the

wreckage-strewn floor, its tentacles waving and groping for more beings to toss aside from its inexorable path.

Jack levelled his gun and fired.

A fiery bolt of pure energy whizzed through the air and burst in the middle of the hideous green thing.

Instantly, a sound like a steam-boiler exploding filled the room. The monstrous plant– as the watchers now realised it to be – writhed and shook and gibbered as if with human rage. But still it advanced!

A hand tugged at Jack's sleeve.

'Captain Weston! Captain Weston! There's only one hope – we've got to reach the door you came through before the creature does.'

Jack recognized the chief scientist of the establishment, Professor Harmer.

'But that – that thing will burst through the wall just as it did before,' snapped Jack.

'Then we must blow up this section of the research station,' Harmer shouted. 'It's our only chance. This is the plant-life we have been experimenting with. The job was going according to plan when, just before the convicts escaped, one of my junior technicians discovered that it had broken loose from the bed in which it was planted. The continual bombardment of gamma rays had changed it– changed it beyond belief!' A look of sheer horror flickered across the scientist's face. 'I believe it has the power to think!'

Jack fired another burst at the monstrous mass.

'Right, men!' he yelled. 'Make for the door! Slim and I will keep it at bay!'

The two men kept up a furious withering fire of energy-bolts as the rest of the party dashed for the door. Then they followed. By now, the weed had reached the centre of the room. It seemed to sense where the fugitives were going. An assortment of tentacles sprang outwards to catch its prey.

And as Jack sprang for the door, a violent green tentacle whipped round his neck and threw him headlong to the floor.

'This way, Captain!' roared Hewitt, firing rapidly into the centre of the mass.

But now another tentacle had licked over Jack's face, a second caught at his legs and arms and yet another curled round his waist and tugged him towards the huge quivering centre of the monstrous creature.

Sick with horror, Jack found himself being dragged bodily towards his doom.

With a last effort, he wrenched his gun hand free and, as he was pulled into the huge wet shadow of the monster's maw, he fired straight up into the wriggling horrible mass – blast after blast.

A hissing squeal of rage erupted from the creature – and its grip slackened. Gasping, Jack wrenched himself free and flung himself through the open door, which was clanged shut by Hewitt.

The two men sprinted down the corridor. Already, the plant-creature was making a furious assault on the wall behind them.

Within seconds it seemed, the two had passed through the airlock and were outside in the half-light of the lunar surface. Harmer's voice came through Jack's helmet receiver.

'You are about to witness an astonishing phenomenon, Captain.' His voice was calm now. 'We have fixed a small charge to the outer hull of the research dome. When detonated, it will tear a small hole in the wall. You follow?'

'Sure, Prof.,' said Jack grimly. 'Because there is an artificial atmosphere inside the dome and no air out here, the whole building will tear itself apart – and the creature with it!'

The party of men were moving as fast as they could towards the refuelling depots.

'Precisely,' said Harmer briskly. 'We have found that the plant growth is able to exist in a very thin atmosphere. Let us see what happens when it is exposed to no air at all.' He pressed a button on a small control box in his hand.

Instantly, a flash of white light showed itself briefly in the blackness of the dome's wall. And then soundlessly, horribly, the whole dome burst apart.

Chunks of concrete exploded away from the Moon's surface and hurtled into space. Others, not so heavy, reached the end of their impetus and floated downwards on to the lunar crags and craters yards away.

Bits of leathery plant-growth fluttered to the ground around the stunned group of men.

Two hours later, order had been restored to the Lunar Colony.

Inside the canteen of the repair depot, Jack Weston sipped at a steaming mug of black coffee.

Professor Harmer came in.

'The remaining convicts have been rounded up, Captain, with the help of your crew,' he said. 'All that remains now is for the Earth government to build me a new research station.'

Jack banged his mug down on the table. 'Come on, men, let's go. I'll bet General Carstairs is having forty blue fits waiting to hear my report on this little spot of fun and games!'

In Deadly Danger

A vital stage in the American Apollo Moon Flight programme was to carry out a successful space rendezvous between two orbiting satellites and join them together.

Neil Armstrong, the first man to tread the surface of the moon, and another astronaut, David Scott, were awarded the task of first performing this tricky task, namely to track down a specially modified Agena-D booster rocket (see left in the illustration) and perform the docking manoeuvre.

The Agena duly arrived in orbit, Scott and Armstrong were blasted off in their space capsule and managing to line up with the docking collar on the Agena, gently nudged their capsule into it.

Now to free the capsule from the Agena. As they fired their thruster jets and the capsule left the Agena, the capsule lurched out of control and began to tumble and spin violently. The No. 8 thruster jet would not shut off and consequently the capsule was spinning uncontrollably.

Calmly the astronauts at once switched control of the Agena rocket back to the scientists at the control centre on Earth and brought the capsule under control by using a separate set of thruster jets, normally used to control the spacecraft during re-entry of the Earth's atmosphere. They succeeded and safely returned to Earth. Their quick thinking had undoubtedly saved their lives.

War Games in Space

Two Russian satellites were manoeuvring in space. They were playing a kind of war game in which one was the hunter and the other its prey.

The hunter circled the victim as if examining it. Then it used a camera to 'shoot' its victim.

At least that is the interpretation western observers put on this 'game' in space. And they were aghast at the implications, which suggested that if a Space Control Headquarters can manoeuvre two space craft close enough to each other so that one can photograph its companion, Space Control can also order one to fire a destructive charge at the other.

The possibility gives rise to a vision of a far more frightening form of warfare taking place far above the Earth in outer space . . . one in which an early warning satellite, 'killed' by a laser beam would fail to detect an invading force . . . in which a space shuttle could use mechanical claws to grab an enemy satellite and pull it into its vast cargo bay . . . in which one satellite could turn another into a molten mass of wreckage.

Crazy? Illogical? Far-fetched? Perhaps it seems so, but it could all happen in the future, according to space experts who have been studying the possibilities of extra-terrestrial warfare.

To shoot down a satellite seems a waste of effort. Why should anyone want to do that? The reason, simply, is that satellites are a nation's first line of defence – they are its skyborne eyes which give warning of an impending attack. To destroy them leaves a defending nation at the mercy of its attackers. An aggressive nation could cripple its opponents' forces in a very short time without having to sink a ship or knock a plane out of the sky.

Years ago, the Russians realized this and began developing a satellite able to smash intruding foreign satellites to smithereens.

It is no secret that satellites carry explosive charges that can be detonated upon a radio command from Earth. The object of this is to destroy satellites that have moved out of their orbit, whose instruments have ceased to function or are otherwise no longer useful.

In 1977, two American satellites encountered a strange phenomenon while passing over Soviet territory.

One American satellite was an early-warning surveillance satellite designed to detect any warlike activity. The other was its message-relay satellite. Somehow the surveillance satellite's 'eyes' were put out of action and its accompanying satellite made completely useless.

The American explanation is that highly sensitive 'eyes' on their satellite were blinded by the brilliance of the glare of flares from a natural gas pipeline. But sceptical scientists doubted whether the flares would have been bright enough to have this effect. They wondered whether a high-powered laser beam from Earth could have done the damage.

To protect their satellites, the Americans fitted them with alarm systems which can send a warning to Earth if they are attacked by another satellite.

On TV screens on Earth, watchers are able to see the attackers because the satellites have very efficient TV cameras and high-powered lights. They also have the rocket power and extra fuel to escape from their attackers.

Backing these up are suicide satellites that would get rid of an enemy by flying close to it and exploding.

Other ideas proposed in America include the use of satellites which release explosives in the path of an enemy and the employment of space shuttles with big cargo bays. They would snatch the satellites out of space and scoop them into its bay.

Treaties by Russia and America ban weapons from space and leave spy satellites unmolested.

At this moment in time, a war in space is something nobody could win. There could be only losers and no victors. Perhaps this is why it may never happen.

Project Venus

If there is one planet other than our own where it might be possible for human beings to live it is Venus. As it is today, however, Venus, approximately the same size as Earth, would be an impossible place for any of us to live. At the surface it has a temperature much hotter than a cooker oven when the heat regulo is turned on fully.

When rain falls on Venus it turns to steam immediately when it strikes the red-hot surface. Because of this, Venus is covered completely with a thick blanket of cloud. From Venus both the Sun during the day and the Moon at night would be invisible.

Engineers way back in 1971 hit upon an ingenious way of making Venus habitable for human beings, the idea being to 'seed' Venus with plant life. The atmosphere on Venus consists mainly of carbon dioxide. On Earth the oxygen we breathe is almost entirely supplied by plants, which use the green chemical compound called 'Chlorophyll' to manufacture oxygen from carbon dioxide in our atmosphere.

Plants used to 'sow life' on Venus would probably be tiny single-celled organisms called Algae, which are found in their billions on the surfaces of ponds.

By using radio-control from Earth, rockets with 'nose cones' filled with algae would be fired from satellites down into the atmosphere of Venus. The 'nose cones' would automatically break open seeding the Venus atmosphere with algae. As they multiplied, the algae would make oxygen from the carbon dioxide. As they grew, drifting about in the clouds, more and more oxygen would be produced. The atmosphere would gradually cool down and more and more rain would fall. Finally the surface would cool and rivers begin to flow. Lakes would form and fresh rivers would be born carrying more and more water down to the new born fresh water sea.

The whole idea is, of course, speculation. Adopted, one would have to 'wait and see' – but then that is a term that is so often applied to experiments in space.